T0198522

Changed by Christmas

Let the Birth of Jesus Transform your Life

SHERRY MYERS

WESTBOW
PRESS®
A DIVISION OF THOMAS NELSON
& ZONDERVAN

WestBow Press books may be ordered through booksellers or by contacting:

WestBow Press
A Division of Thomas Nelson & Zondervan
1663 Liberty Drive
Bloomington, IN 47403
www.westbowpress.com
1 (866) 928-1240

Because of the dynamic nature of the Internet, any web addresses or
links contained in this book may have changed since publication and
may no longer be valid. The views expressed in this work are solely those
of the author and do not necessarily reflect the views of the publisher,
and the publisher hereby disclaims any responsibility for them.

Any people depicted in stock imagery provided by Getty Images are
models, and such images are being used for illustrative purposes only.
Certain stock imagery © Getty Images.

All Scripture passages, unless otherwise noted, are taken from The Holy
Bible, English Standard Version® (ESV®), Copyright © 2001 by Crossway,
a publishing ministry of Good News Publishers. All rights reserved.

Scripture quotations marked (NIV) are taken from the Holy Bible, New
International Version®, NIV®. Copyright © 1973, 1978, 1984, 2011 by Biblica,
Inc.™ Used by permission of Zondervan. All rights reserved worldwide. www.
zondervan.com The "NIV" and "New International Version" are trademarks
registered in the United States Patent and Trademark Office by Biblica, Inc.™

ISBN: 978-1-9736-6823-7 (sc)
ISBN: 978-1-9736-6923-4 (hc)
ISBN: 978-1-9736-6822-0 (e)

Library of Congress Control Number: 2019909266

Print information available on the last page.

WestBow Press rev. date: 8/9/2019

CONTENTS

To my husband and soul mate, Tommy Myers, who models the love of God with a quiet strength and sacrificial love while providing godly leadership of our family;

to my daddy, Ralph Jones, who taught me the Word of God and helped me develop a love for studying it and applying it to my life; and

to my mother, Dot Jones, who modeled Christlikeness through her love for her family and spiritual gifts of hospitality and service.

I would like to thank our children and their
mates for their support in this project:

Kristin and Brett Myers

Christie and Brandon Brown

INTRODUCTION

In my study of the birth of Jesus, what became so real to me was how very much this story changed history forever. Humanity was changed forever. Think about it...If Jesus had not been born to live and die for the sins of humanity, we would still be sacrificing animals for our sins, we who are Christians would not have the full-time presence of the Holy Spirit; we would not have direct access to God through Jesus; we would not have seen the fulfillment of the love of God. Jesus was sent to earth to literally and fully change lives. We who accept this wonderful Christmas gift of Jesus can be forever changed by His presence if we allow Him that freedom.

This Bible study is a gift that God gave me the first Christmas my daddy spent in heaven. He had passed away in April 1999 and had always been to my brother and me a godly father who emulated God's character, and one who made it easy for us to understand the love of God because we saw it in him. He loved us unconditionally, he sacrificed for us, he taught us the Bible, but, most importantly, he lived the Word.

On the afternoon of Thanksgiving that year, I remember standing on our back deck as I looked toward the mountains, asking God, "How can we get through this Christmas season without Daddy?" Christmas had always been a very big deal with our family, including my parents, grandparents, and extended family. My mother and grandmothers loved cooking delicious meals for everyone and decorating their houses to reflect the joy and celebration of the season. The thought of going through the season without my daddy was more than I could imagine. As soon as I prayed that prayer, though, I knew God was telling me that He was with me and that this year I needed to celebrate this being my daddy's first Christmas in heaven instead of our first Christmas without him. What a wonderful thought that seemed, that I could celebrate my daddy's presence with God, with Jesus, and with all the saints who had gone before him, and what a glorious celebration that must be with all the saints before the throne of God, singing glorious praises to Him and His Son, who had made it possible for them to be there!

As a result, I decided to study the Christmas story that year at a much deeper level, a reflection of my daddy's love for the Word. I studied a part of it each day and God made it so much more alive for me than it had ever been. It was the most spiritually rich Christmas I had ever spent. What a wonderful gift God had given me—a deeper love and appreciation for the Word in a way that I had seen in my daddy! It was like a Christmas present from God in honor of my daddy. Only God could turn what otherwise would have been a very sad season into the most joyous Christmas season I had ever experienced as He used what was my daddy's passion—knowing, teaching, and practicing the Word of God—to transform me and give me a love for writing Bible studies. This was the first one I wrote, and I have updated it over the years. I have also written several other Bible studies since first writing this one, none of them on my own, but as simply gifts from God. It's a joy to share this study with you. I pray you find hope and inspiration through these words and that you experience a renewed awe of the true meaning of the Christmas season.

Prologue

Before we begin our look at the birth of Jesus with its many surrounding details, we must point out that this really is not the beginning of the story of Jesus. We see Jesus mentioned in Genesis 1:26a, which says, "Let us make man in our image, after our likeness," and in Genesis 3:15 when God told the serpent, "And I will put enmity between you and the woman, and between your offspring and her offspring; he shall bruise your head, and you shall bruise his heel." God had His plan in place when He created the earth and all that's in it. He knew that man would fall into temptation with the free will that He would give him, so He planned a way that the relationship between Him and man could be restored. It was a glorious plan, but it was also a painful plan because it would cause His only Son to leave the glory and comfort of heaven to live the life of a man on earth, experiencing tremendous pain and suffering.

Many Old Testament prophets foretold the birth of Jesus. Isaiah was one of them. As recorded in Isaiah 7:14, he told the people, "Therefore, the Lord himself will give you a sign. Behold, the virgin shall conceive and bear a son, and shall call his name Immanuel." Then Isaiah 9:6 records these additional words of prophecy: "For to us a child is born, to us a son is given; and the government shall be upon his shoulder, and his name shall be called Wonderful Counselor, Mighty God, Everlasting Father, Prince of Peace." Isaiah 10 describes the difficulties the Israelites faced and would continue to face from their enemies, but chapter 11 verse 1 gives them hope: "There shall come forth a shoot from the stump of Jesse, and a branch from his roots shall bear fruit." God would bring the true King from the line of David.

The place of Jesus's birth was also prophesied in the Old Testament. Micah 5:2 says, "But you, O Bethlehem Ephrathah, who are too little to be among the clans of Judah, from you shall come forth for me one who is to be ruler in Israel, whose coming forth is from of old, from ancient days."

This is only a sampling of prophecies of the coming Messiah recorded in the Old Testament. The story of Christmas, as we will examine it, is simply the fulfilling of the promised Messiah who would teach the heart of God, would sacrifice His life for the payment of the sins of humanity, and would be raised to heaven to sit at the right hand of the throne of God to rule over His kingdom.

Now let us open the curtain on this glorious story, the greatest story ever told and that ever was.

Day One—Preparing the Way

¹¹And there appeared to him an angel of the Lord standing on the right side of the altar of incense. ¹² And Zechariah was troubled when he saw him, and fear fell upon him. ¹³ But the angel said to him, "Do not be afraid, Zechariah, for your prayer has been heard, and your wife Elizabeth will bear you a son, and you shall call his name John. ¹⁴ And you will have joy and gladness, and many will rejoice at his birth, ¹⁵ for he will be great before the Lord. And he must not drink wine or strong drink, and he will be filled with the Holy Spirit, even from his mother's womb. ¹⁶ And he will turn many of the children of Israel to the Lord their God, ¹⁷ and he will go before him in the spirit and power of Elijah, to turn the hearts of the fathers to the children, and the disobedient to the wisdom of the just, to make ready for the Lord a people prepared."

—Luke 1:11–17

The above passage gives the account of the angel appearing to Zechariah and foretelling the birth of John the Baptist. The angel told him these things:

1. His prayer had been heard. Elizabeth would bear a son, and they were to name him John.

2. John would bring joy and gladness to Zechariah and Elizabeth.
3. Many would rejoice at his birth.
4. He would be great in the sight of the Lord.
5. He must not drink wine or strong drink, and he would be filled with the Holy Spirit from birth.
6. He would turn many of the children of Israel to God.
7. He would turn the hearts of the fathers to the children and the disobedient to the wisdom of God.
8. He would prepare the people for the coming of Jesus.

Let's consider first why God chose to use Zechariah and Elizabeth for such a task as bringing into the world and parenting the one who would prepare the way for the ministry of the Son of God. Luke 1:5–6 says, "⁵In the days of Herod, king of Judea, there was a priest named Zechariah, of the division of Abijah. And he had a wife from the daughters of Aaron, and her name was Elizabeth. ⁶And they were both righteous before God, walking blamelessly in all the commandments and statutes of the Lord." Write verse 6 in your own words.

Do you see how Luke describes being "righteous before God"? He defines it as "walking blamelessly in all the commandments and statutes of the Lord." So Elizabeth and Zechariah had been faithful to God. Then verse 7 says this: "But they had no child, because Elizabeth was barren, and both were advanced in years." Even though they had been faithful to God, their prayers for a child had not been answered affirmatively, and they were both considered beyond the age of childbearing; however, they continued to faithfully serve God. God, nevertheless, had a plan for them that was to be fulfilled only in His time. Remember that nothing is impossible with God. Can you imagine the delight Zechariah and Elizabeth felt at this news! We get a glimpse at Elizabeth's heart as recorded in Luke 1:25: "²⁵Thus the Lord has done for me in the days when he looked on me, to take away my reproach among people."

Look back at our list of the truths the angel told Zechariah. In summary, John was the answer to his parents' prayers, he would bring joy and gladness to them, he would have a much more far-reaching impact than just his family, even God would consider him great, he would be filled with the Holy Spirit even from birth, he would bring many people back to God, and he would prepare the way for the coming of the Messiah. There had been many great prophets, but surely Zechariah and Elizabeth knew that their son would be among the greatest prophets who would ever live.

We certainly aren't called of God to fulfill John the Baptist's role specifically, but we are called of God as His children to share the Gospel of Jesus and prepare the way for others to know him personally. Let's then apply some of these truths to our lives.

1. God heard the prayers of Zechariah and Elizabeth for a child. God hears our prayers just as He heard their prayers for a child. God had a plan the whole time, and His answer that Elizabeth had thought was "no" was actually "yes—in My time." God's ways are always best; after all, He created us, and He has the only plan that really matters. When we allow His plan to become ours, we are better able to fulfill His will. Zechariah made the mistake of asking the angel, "How can I be sure of this?" which caused him to lose his voice until after John was born. This tells us that God takes our unbelief very seriously. Even though we will most likely never be visited by an angel in this lifetime to tell us that God is going to answer our prayers, we can have the assurance that He will because He tells us in His Word that He hears our prayers and is faithful to answer them. Psalm 145:13b says, "The LORD is faithful in all his words and kind in all his works."

Do you struggle with believing that God hears your prayers? If so, pause and pray right now, asking God to help you believe that He hears and will answer your prayers. Write out your thoughts.

_____

_____

2. John brought joy and gladness to his parents because he chose to follow God's magnificent plan for his life. He's the only person mentioned in scripture who was indwelled by the Holy Spirit from birth. John was born for a specific purpose, and we see in scripture that he focused on that purpose and fulfilled it to the nth degree. We can also be a joy and delight to those around us when we allow the Holy Spirit full rein in our lives.

    Can you say that you have brought joy and gladness to your parents and, more importantly, to God? Write your thoughts below.

    _____

    _____

3. John the Baptist was great in the eyes of God because he aligned his will with God's will and was focused solely on fulfilling what God called him to do. We are filled with the same Holy Spirit from the time of our spiritual births. Think about that: the same Holy Spirit that filled John the Baptist and enabled him to serve his purpose lives in us to enable us to serve our purpose. How can we be as focused as John was in aligning our will to God's? The answer has to do with surrendering our will to His. If you surrender your will to God's will and ask Him for wisdom through the power of His Holy Spirit, He will help you see clearly His will for you and then enable you to simply obey. Simple obedience may not always be easy, but it's the key to a blessed and meaningful life.

Are there any changes you need to make to be more closely aligned with God's purpose for your life?

_____

_____

4. John brought many people to Jesus and prepared the way for Jesus's ministry. As disciples or followers of Jesus, we also have the responsibility of bringing others to Him and preparing the way for others to know Him. Our lives should be so aligned with God's character that those around us are prepared to hear us tell them about Jesus. Recall how the angel described this preparing the way: "to turn the hearts of the fathers to the children and the disobedient to the wisdom of the just." These are things only God can do, but He chose to use people as His vessels through whom He would do it. **The main way that we can prepare others to hear the Gospel is by living lives before them that are consistent with God's character.** That's what makes people open to hear about Jesus and what He did for them. Exodus 20:7 says, "You shall not take the name of the Lord your God in vain, for the Lord will not hold him guiltless who takes his name in vain." We all know the traditional interpretation of this verse, but I believe it also means to not take or carry God's name in a worthless manner (in vain). If you say you're a Christian and yet do not behave in a manner worthy of God, you are taking God's name around with you for not only a worthless manner, but to His detriment. We who call ourselves Christians should be constantly mindful that we represent Him in everything we do. Be prepared to live in such a way that will lead others to Jesus by aligning yourself with God every day. He has a plan for your life just as He had a plan for John the Baptist.

Consider how you measure up in preparing the way for people around you to know God. Are there changes you need to make?

_____

_____

Meditate today on this part of Luke 1:17: "And he will go before him ... to make ready for the Lord a people prepared." Throughout the day, ask God to help you be very aware of His presence in your life and to fill you with the power of the Holy Spirit so that you, too, are able to prepare the way for people to hear the good news of what Jesus has done for them.

Notes

Day Two—A Life Foretold

²⁶ In the sixth month the angel Gabriel was sent from God to a city of Galilee named Nazareth, ²⁷to a virgin betrothed to a man whose name was Joseph, of the house of David. And the virgin's name was Mary. ²⁸ And he came to her and said, "Greetings, O favored one, the Lord is with you!" ²⁹ But she was greatly troubled at the saying, and tried to discern what sort of greeting this might be. ³⁰ And the angel said to her, "Do not be afraid, Mary, for you have found favor with God. ³¹ And behold, you will conceive in your womb and bear a son, and you shall call his name Jesus. ³² He will be great and will be called the Son of the Most High. And the Lord God will give to him the throne of his father David, ³³ and he will reign over the house of Jacob forever, and of his kingdom there will be no end."

—Luke 1:26–33

Consider what the angel Gabriel told Mary about the Son she would have:

1. _____ would be his name.
2. He would be great and would be called the _____ _____ _____ _____ _____.

3. He would be given the throne of _____ and would reign over the house of Jacob.
4. Of His kingdom there would be _____ _____.

If I had been Mary, this is probably how I would have taken that message: "I will name my son Jesus; He will be looked upon as great and everyone will know him as the Son of the Most High God; he will be the next king." However, God is the author and creator of the universe; therefore, He sees the whole picture, including eternity. To Him, evidently, what was important was that Jesus would become a man, that He would do what God sent Him to do, which would be to give His life for the sins of all humanity, that He would be called the Son of the Most High, and that He would reign forever.

This is God's summation of Jesus's life and purpose. As difficult as Jesus's physical life on earth was, those difficulties were not mentioned by God in the summation of His life. That tells me that they paled in comparison to the whole scheme of things. What was important was what Jesus did and the end result. His purpose was to teach the mind of God, die on the cross for the sins of the world, and then, because of His obedience to God's plan for Him, ascend to heaven where He would reign on His throne. Jesus's goal was to reign as King in heaven forever. His earthly ministry was to begin building that kingdom. Therefore, He taught people everywhere He went and set up an earthly ministry through His disciples. He received His strength from God, and He was obedient to God in everything, even death on the cross. Jesus's earthly life was totally in line with His eternal life. In eternity there are no regrets for Jesus. He did with His physical life all that had been the will of God for Him.

If an angel had appeared to your parents foretelling your birth, what do you think would have been said to them?

_____

_____

If an angel had appeared to my parents before I was born and had given them a similar message concerning me, it would probably have been something like "You will have a daughter, and you will name her Sherry. She will be called a child of the Most High. The Lord God will be with her, and she will live in His kingdom forever." You see, what is important to God about my life is the decision that I make in this physical life to accept Jesus's sacrifice so that I can be called His child, my obedience to Him in following His plan for my life, then finally my living in His presence for all of eternity. All the difficulties I face would not be mentioned because God is in control and they're not difficulties to Him at all. What is important is that I am obedient and that God is glorified in all that I do.

My focus every day should be that—to obey God and to glorify God. My eyes should be fixed on the prize at the end of the race—to live in heaven with Jesus. This is described best in Hebrews 12:1–2: "¹Therefore, since we are surrounded by so great a cloud of witnesses, let us also lay aside every weight, and sin which clings so closely, and let us run with endurance the race that is set before us, ²looking to Jesus, the founder and perfecter of our faith, who for the joy that was set before him endured the cross, despising the shame, and is seated at the right hand of the throne of God."

If I set my eyes on Jesus every day and my focus on pleasing Him and spending eternity in heaven, my thoughts turn to "What will it take for God to be able to say to me, 'Well done, good and faithful servant. Enter into the joy of your master'?" If I truly love and obey God and follow His example, I will exemplify the fruit of His Spirit, and I will share Him with others, lead as many as are willing to a saving knowledge of Him, and then disciple them. **If my goal is to spend eternity worshiping and praising God and serving Him alongside those whom I have brought**

with me, then my earthly ministry should be in line with that goal. I know that I will not get to heaven without regrets, but I can choose each day to be obedient to God for that day, to love Him with all my heart, soul, mind, and strength, to share Him with others, and to disciple those whom He places in my circle of influence. If I seek God and His righteousness each day, then there will be fewer regrets when I stand before Him in all His glory.

When you think about your eternity, are you absolutely sure that you will spend it in heaven? _____ If you answered no and you would like to accept Jesus's sacrifice on the cross as payment for your sins, pray the following prayer, meaning it with all your heart:

> Lord God, I confess my sins to You and acknowledge that I am unable to save myself. Right now I claim Jesus's death on the cross as payment for my sins, and I place my faith and trust in You to save me so that I can have fellowship with You. I realize that this is the beginning of my eternal life, and I thank you for saving me and allowing me to have eternal life through Jesus. In Jesus's holy name, I pray, amen.

If you have sincerely prayed this prayer either just now or at a previous time in your life, you belong to God, and His Spirit lives in your heart to enable you to live in a way that is pleasing to Him.

Think about the time when you will meet God face to face. What do you think your thoughts will be?

_____

_____

When you think about facing God one day, what do you think will be your biggest regret?

_____

You cannot do anything about the past, but you can do something about the future. Ask God to help you get your physical life more in line with your eternal life. What changes do you believe He is asking you to make?

_____

_____

Will you surrender your will right now to make those changes? Try not to overwhelm yourself by focusing on all the rest of your life. Just focus on surrendering to His will today and take it one day at a time. God will bless you as you follow Him.

Focus today on these words from Hebrews 12:1–2: "Let us run with endurance the race that is set before us, looking to Jesus, the founder and perfecter of our faith." Focus on the impact that Jesus's birth had on all humanity and on your responsibility to follow His teachings so that you, too, can have an impact on those around you. Throughout the day, ask God to help you set your heart on living according to His character, leading others to Him, and discipling those whom God gives you opportunity.

Notes

Day Three—Favored by God

²⁶ In the sixth month the angel Gabriel was sent from God to a city of Galilee named Nazareth, ²⁷ to a virgin betrothed to a man whose name was Joseph, of the house of David. And the virgin's name was Mary. ²⁸ And he came to her and said, "Greetings, O favored one, the Lord is with you!" ²⁹ But she was greatly troubled at the saying, and tried to discern what sort of greeting this might be. ³⁰ And the angel said to her, "Do not be afraid, Mary, for you have found favor with God."

—Luke 1:26–30

The angel made four statements to Mary after the word *greetings*. What were they?

1. _____

2. _____

3. _____

4. _____

Have you ever listened in on someone else's conversation and wished that you were a part of it? Maybe someone was getting confirmation and encouragement of which you would have loved to be the recipient. The angel's words to Mary regarding her finding favor with God are words that we should all long for and pursue with all our hearts.

These words to Mary help us to know the heart of God. Today we will look at other scripture passages that concern favor with God to see what that really means. Genesis 4:3–4 says, "In the course of time Cain brought to the LORD an offering of the fruit of the ground, ⁴and Abel also brought of the firstborn of his flock and of their fat portions. And the LORD had regard for Abel and his offering." Abel brought _____ _____ from his flock and their _____ _____. In other words, Abel gave God the best of the first. As a result, Abel found favor with God.

Do you give God the first and the best of all you have and all you are? Or do you give Him the leftover time, the leftover money, the leftover energy, the leftover devotion? What changes would you have to make to give God the best of your first of everything?

_____

_____

Here's another example of a man who found favor with God. Genesis 6:6–9 says, "And the LORD regretted that he had made man on the earth, and it grieved him to his heart. ⁷So the LORD said, 'I will blot out man whom I have created from the face of the land, man and animals and creeping things and birds of the heavens, for I am sorry that I have made them.' ⁸But Noah found favor in the eyes of the LORD. ⁹These are the generations of Noah. Noah was a righteous man, blameless in his generation. Noah walked with God."

God was grieved by the wickedness He saw in mankind, but there was one light in all that wickedness, and his name was Noah. Verse 8 says that Noah found _____ in the eyes of the Lord. Verse 9 goes on to describe Noah. What reason does verse 9 give for Noah's finding favor with God?

_____

_____

The phrase "Noah walked with God" provides the foundation for Noah's righteousness. If we are to emulate God and His character, we must walk with Him so we can know Him. Examine your life in light of walking with God and write ways you feel you do that and what you could do to walk more closely and more consistently with Him.

_____

_____

_____

Leviticus 26:3–13 gives one of the best descriptions of the cause and effect of God's favor.

> ³If you walk in my statutes and observe my commandments and do them, ⁴then I will give you your rains in their season, and the land shall yield its increase, and the trees of the field shall yield their fruit. ⁵Your threshing shall last to the time of the grape harvest, and the grape harvest shall last to the time for sowing. And you shall eat your bread to the full and dwell in your land securely. ⁶I will give peace in the land, and you shall lie down, and none shall make you afraid. And I will remove harmful beasts from the land, and the sword shall not go through your land. ⁷You shall chase your enemies, and they shall fall before you by the sword. ⁸Five of you shall chase a hundred, and a hundred of you shall chase ten thousand, and your enemies shall fall before you by the sword. ⁹I will turn to you and make you fruitful and multiply you and will confirm my covenant with you. ¹⁰You shall eat old store long kept, and you shall clear out the old to make way for the new. ¹¹I will make my dwelling among you, and my soul

shall not abhor you. [12] And I will walk among you
and will be your God, and you shall be my people.
[13] I am the LORD your God, who brought you out
of the land of Egypt, that you should not be their
slaves. And I have broken the bars of your yoke
and made you walk erect.

Write below the condition on which God's favor rests as found
in this passage.

_____

Next list the effects of His favor.

_____
_____
_____
_____
_____

We can group the effects discussed into four areas:

1. The harvest would be plentiful.
2. The people would enjoy peace as they experience victory
   over their enemies.
3. They would have many descendants.
4. God would walk among them.

Verse 13 concludes with the following quote from God: "And I
have broken the bars of your yoke and made you walk erect." God is
the same today as He was then. Not only does He walk with those
who are obedient to His commands, but also today He breaks the
bars of their yokes and enables them to walk with heads held high.
He wants to free you from the bondage of your sin and allow you
to live a life of peace and freedom. The only condition is obedience

to His commands, which are given so that we can enjoy the best of the feast that He's prepared for us.

One key to obedience is spending time with Him in the study of His Word and in prayer so that we are able to know His character and thereby know what He expects. The other key is surrendering our will to His, being willing to forsake our desires for His. I would venture to say that any Christian would say that he would like to find favor in the eyes of God, but not all crave it enough to do what it takes to invest the time to know God's commands and then be willing to obey them. John 14:23 records the words of Jesus that tie together our love for Him and our obedience to His Word. It says, "If anyone loves me, he will keep my word." Therefore, obedience comes out of love for God. **Loving God at a level great enough to cause obedience to Him is the key to finding favor from Him.**

Let's go back now to the angel's words to Mary. The angel told her twice in this announcement that she was favored by God. Look back at the four phrases you listed at the first of today's study. Notice the first and fourth phrases concerned Mary's being favored by God, but notice the two phrases in between those two statements. "The Lord is with you" and "Do not be afraid" are key to one who is highly favored by God. When we have God's favor, we have Him walking with us, and thus, we have nothing to fear because we know that He is in control. It's important to realize this because God never asks us to do something without promising to be with us. His presence means more than any other person's. His being with us doesn't just provide us company; it also enables us to do whatever He asks us to do. What more could we ask?

Mary was just as human as we are, and yet she lived her life in a way that was pleasing to God. He will not ask us to do what He asked Mary to do, but He does, just the same, have a plan for our lives; He has tasks that He wants us to do. If we aren't obedient to Him, we will not find favor with Him and we will miss out on the privilege of being a vessel used by the God of the universe. How sad that would be!

Evaluate your level of obedience. Are there areas of your life in which you are not being obedient to God's commands? _____ If so, what are they, and what will you do about them?

_____

_____

Are you spending enough time with God every day to know His commands? _____ If not, what will you do about that?

_____

_____

Meditate today on the angel's words, "The Lord is with you. Do not be afraid ... you have found favor with God." Throughout the day, ask God to show you what it means to (1) know that He is with you so that you don't have to be afraid of the future and (2) find favor in His eyes. Also throughout the day, thank God for sending His Son to be born in the flesh so that you are able to know Him, walk with Him, and find favor with Him.

Notes

DAY FOUR—A HUMBLE SERVANT

³⁴And Mary said to the angel, "How will this be, since I am a virgin?" ³⁵And the angel answered her, "The Holy Spirit will come upon you, and the power of the Most High will overshadow you; therefore the child to be born will be called holy—the Son of God. ³⁶And behold, your relative Elizabeth in her old age has also conceived a son, and this is the sixth month with her who was called barren. ³⁷For nothing will be impossible with God." ³⁸And Mary said, "Behold, I am the servant of the Lord; let it be to me according to your word." And the angel departed from her.

—Luke 1:34–38

What strikes me in this passage is how willing Mary was to accept this strange and incredible message. She had to know the embarrassment she would face at the knowledge that she was expecting a child and was only engaged to be married. Think about it: she was being spoken to by an angel who gave her a message from God! The only question Mary had for the angel was "How will this be since I am a virgin?" Notice the word *will*, which indicates that she knew it would happen, she just didn't understand the how of it. God's power is unlimited; He can do whatever He chooses to do. Notice that Mary's question did not involve a selfish thought. It would have been understandable for

Mary to have asked something like "What about Joseph? He'll think I've been unfaithful to him." Then, "How will I explain it to my family, friends, and our community? They'll never believe me. I'll be stoned to death!" But Mary did not ask all these questions. From Mary's next comment, it appears that she simply accepted the angel's words and did not waste time arguing and deliberating it with him. She left all these issues in the hands of God. Mary simply said, "I am the servant of the Lord; let it be to me according to your word." No argument. No more questions.

The most logical explanation for Mary's response is that she had just been in the presence of an angel who spoke to her from God—the only true and living God, the creator and sustainer of the universe. Think of the last time, hopefully recently, that God spoke to you. If you are a child of God, His Holy Spirit lives within you, and God speaks to you through Him. Our Bible study and prayer time should be so intimate in fellowship with God that we hear His voice, although sometimes we hear Him more clearly than others. God isn't limited to just our Bible study and prayer time, though. He can speak to us anytime He chooses. When God speaks to me, it is an eye-opening experience, and I'm not led to question Him; I just want to obey Him, trust Him, and praise Him because He is God and I know He loves me.

So going back to Mary's message from the angel, let's look at the key to her faith. It is found in what is called "Mary's Song" in verses 46–49. This passage says, "⁴⁶And Mary said, 'My soul magnifies the Lord, ⁴⁷and my spirit rejoices in God my Savior, ⁴⁸for he has looked on the humble estate of his servant. For behold, from now on all generations will call me blessed; ⁴⁹for he who is mighty has done great things for me, and holy is his name.'"

Deep in Mary's soul was a desire to put God's glory above all else. The soul is the core of who we are, and it is the part of us that continues to live beyond our last physical breath. The soul is also the seat of our emotions, values, desires, and passions. Therefore, from the core of who she was and with all her passion,

Mary glorified, praised, and exalted God. What reason did she give for this?

_____

_____

Mary also said that God had "looked on the humble estate of his servant." This humility God saw in Mary is likely a main reason He chose her to bear His Son. Because His Word is timeless, we know that God still today looks at His humble servant with pleasure. Consider what it means to be God's humble servant. A humble servant does the following:

1. Follows orders exactly as they are given. (Doesn't do a task his own way.)
2. Considers his master's needs and desires more important than his own.
3. Looks for ways to serve even when not asked. (Goes above and beyond the call of duty.)
4. Is always available.
5. Is loyal to his master.
6. Is obedient to every command of his master.
7. Desires the recognition and glory to go to his master, is not interested in getting recognition or glory for himself.

Now consider each of these things concerning your relationship with God. Give evidence or lack of evidence concerning each one.

1. _____
2. _____
3. _____
4. _____
5. _____
6. _____
7. _____

Does your soul glorify God in all you do? Do you humble yourself before Him daily as His servant? Do you accept God's will for your life without questioning Him? Spend a few moments reflecting on these questions and asking God to help you live in a way that pleases Him.

Meditate today on Mary's words, "I am the servant of the Lord; let it be to me according to your word." Bow your heart to God's authority, humble yourself before Him, and rejoice in Christ your Savior. Then seek to glorify God in all you do today.

Notes

Day Five—Simple Belief

And blessed is she who believed that there would be a
fulfillment of what was spoken to her from the Lord.
—Luke 1:45

L uke recorded Mary's visit to Elizabeth after the angel had told
her that she would be with child. Elizabeth responded with the
statement shown above, blessing Mary for her belief. Mary's faith in
God had to be a part of what led God to find her highly favored. She
was blessed more than any other woman in history. It was said of her
that she believed that what the Lord said to her would be accomplished.
Do we believe that strongly in what God says to us? We have the same
capability of belief that Mary had. She had the same sinful nature that
we have. What's the difference in Mary's belief and yours?

_____

_____

It all comes down to a choice: Do we believe God or not?
Choosing to believe God allows Him to completely work His plan in
us. Choosing not to believe God causes us sleepless nights, anxiety,
and the sickness that results from it, the loss of the privilege to be
used of God, the loss of peace and joy that belongs to us as children
of God, and the losses go on and on. List instances in which you or
others you know have had difficulty believing God.

_____

_____

Read the following passages and write the result of each instance involving unbelief.

Numbers 20:12: "¹²And the LORD said to Moses and Aaron, 'Because you did not believe in me, to uphold me as holy in the eyes of the people of Israel, therefore you shall not bring this assembly into the land that I have given them.'"

Matthew 13:55–58: "⁵⁵Is not this the carpenter's son? Is not his mother called Mary? And are not his brothers James and Joseph and Simon and Judas? ⁵⁶And are not all his sisters with us? Where then did this man get all these things?" ⁵⁷And they took offense at him. But Jesus said to them, "A prophet is not without honor except in his hometown and in his own household." ⁵⁸And he did not do many mighty works there, because of their unbelief."

Matthew 17:18–20: "¹⁸And Jesus rebuked the demon and it came out of him, and the boy was healed instantly. ¹⁹Then the disciples came to Jesus privately and said, 'Why could we not cast it out?' ²⁰He said to them, 'Because of your little faith. For truly, I say to you, if you have faith like a grain of mustard seed, you will say to this mountain, 'Move from here to there,' and it will move, and nothing will be impossible for you.'"

John 20:27–29: "²⁷Then he said to Thomas, 'Put your finger here, and see my hands; and put out your hand, and place it in my side. Do not disbelieve, but believe.' ²⁸Thomas answered him, 'My Lord and my God!' ²⁹Jesus said to him, 'Have you believed because you have seen me? Blessed are those who have not seen and yet have believed.'"

Sherry Myers

Hebrews 11:6: "And without faith it is impossible to please him, for whoever would draw near to God must believe that he exists and that he rewards those who seek him."

_____

John 3:18: "Whoever believes in him is not condemned, but whoever does not believe is condemned already, because he has not believed in the name of the only Son of God."

_____

Turn these situations around, and you see the following benefits of believing God:

1. Experience the promised land—the fulfillment of God's ultimate plan for your life.
2. See the miracles of God.
3. Be used of God.
4. Be blessed by God and experience the joy that He gives.
5. Be pleasing to God.
6. Experience eternal life.

God didn't call us to bear the Savior of the world physically as He did Mary, but, nevertheless, He has a plan that He holds us just as responsible for following. He has a specific purpose for every believer. All believers, though, have a central purpose that binds us together—we are all called to bear Jesus in a way different from Mary but just as important. Mary carried Jesus in her body and bore Him so that the world could know Him as Savior. We, too, carry Him with us wherever we go so that those around us can see Him in us and come to know Him as their Savior. Do you really believe that God, the creator and sustainer of the universe, can use you as His vessel to accomplish His purpose? _____ Why or why not?

_____

The basis for believing God is studying His Word. One of the beatitudes says, "Blessed are those who hunger and thirst for righteousness, for they shall be satisfied" (Matthew 5:6). Ask God to give you that hunger and thirst for His Word so you can have the foundation for living a life of righteousness. We must first know it before we can believe it and grasp it.

We don't know every detail of God's plan for our lives, just as Mary didn't know every detail of God's plan for her life. But just like Mary, we are responsible for believing that what God tells us will be accomplished and for taking it one step at a time. Mary would have driven herself crazy if she had tried to figure out the whole plan. We waste precious time trying to second guess God and figure out the "why" or "how" of His plan when we should be simply trusting Him and pressing on with what we know to do today. God will take care of tomorrow.

Just trust God. You, too, will be blessed when you believe that what God has said to you will be accomplished. **Mary's belief enabled her to bear the physical body of Jesus. Our belief enables us to bear the Spirit of Jesus. Mary's belief was that God could do through her whatever He willed to do. The same can be true for us.**

Mary wasn't the only one who was asked to exercise simple, yet incredible belief in this glorious message. Consider Joseph's predicament. We read this in Matthew 1:18-25:

> [18]Now the birth of Jesus Christ took place in this way. When his mother Mary had been betrothed to Joseph, before they came together she was found to be with child from the Holy Spirit. [19]And her husband Joseph, being a just man and unwilling to put her to shame, resolved to divorce her quietly. [20]But as he considered these things, behold, an angel of the Lord appeared to him in a dream,

saying, "Joseph, son of David, do not fear to take Mary as your wife, for that which is conceived in her is from the Holy Spirit. [21]She will bear a son, and you shall call his name Jesus, for he will save his people from their sins." [22]All this took place to fulfill what the Lord had spoken by the prophet: [23]"Behold, the virgin shall conceive and bear a son, and they shall call his name Immanuel" (which means, God with us). [24]When Joseph woke from sleep, he did as the angel of the Lord commanded him: he took his wife, [25]but knew her not until she had given birth to a son. And he called his name Jesus.

With the appearance of the angel, Joseph's heart and mind went from divorcing Mary quietly to believing her story and the angel's message and taking her as his wife. God made His message very clear to Joseph and Mary through the angels' visits. You may be thinking, "I'd believe, too, if an angel appeared and spoke to me!" However, we who are believers have the Holy Spirit living inside us all the time to speak to us and guide us. He can change our hearts and minds just as He did Joseph's. We just have to listen to Him with a willing heart and mind.

Joseph and Mary were common people and yet God had a miraculous plan for their lives and He used them in a powerful way. We should never, then, doubt God's ability to use us or anyone else for His purpose. God's kingdom is not at all about our ability—it's all about God and His ability to accomplish whatever He desires. Our part is to, out of simple belief, love Him and be devoted to carrying out His will for us.

Meditate today on Luke 1:45: "And blessed is she who believed that there would be a fulfillment of what was spoken to her from the Lord." Throughout the day, ask God to help you believe that He will do what He says He will do. Also throughout the day, thank God for sending His Son so that you can believe on Him and bear His Spirit with you at all times.

Notes

DAY SIX—DIFFICULTIES

[56]And Mary remained with her about three months and returned to her home.

—Luke 1:56

[1]In those days a decree went out from Caesar Augustus that all the world should be registered ... [4]And Joseph also went up from Galilee, from the town of Nazareth, to Judea, to the city of David, which is called Bethlehem, because he was of the house and lineage of David, [5]to be registered with Mary, his betrothed, who was with child.

—Luke 2:1, 4–5

As I read Luke 1 and the beginning of Luke 2, I thought about the fact that we are not told all that happened to Mary between the time she left Zechariah and Elizabeth's home, three months pregnant, to the time she and Joseph traveled to Bethlehem and Jesus was born. Since John the Baptist was born about six months before Jesus, Mary could have stayed until his birth and then left. I wonder, though, why this in-between period was not discussed. It had to be an extremely difficult time for Mary and Joseph as they faced people in their community who did not believe their story. Maybe it is not covered because, even as hard as it was, it all paled in comparison to the rest of the story. We have to gather from Mary's character exemplified in the story of the angel's appearance to her that she, in humility, simply and faithfully trusted God.

As I look back over my life, can I say the same thing? There were so many times I fretted and whined because I did not understand something or just simply failed to trust God. Many times I did finally, after a period of fretting and whining, decide to trust God and accept His plan. An example of that is a situation that I call the cornerstone of my faith.

I had parents who modeled faith in God, but I was a little slow in my own possession of it. In about 1977, I was a single adult, sharing an apartment with a friend. One night my roommate walked into my room and told me she was moving at the end of the month. At first, panic set in, but pretty quickly I decided that I just needed to trust God this time. So I prayed something like this:

"Lord, You know that many times in the past I've tried and tried to work out a difficulty my way, and then when I couldn't, I finally gave it to You, and You worked it out Your way, which was much better than my way. So this time, I'm just going to skip trying to work this out my way, and I'm giving this to You to work out however You see fit. I trust You to do whatever is Your will. You know that I can't afford an apartment by myself, and You also know that I don't know a Christian girl who needs a roommate. But You have the power to work this out, and I'm just asking You to take control of this situation and work it out."

I turned over and went to sleep with complete peace that God had this and that He would work it out. The next morning, I went in to work, and my boss called me into his office. He had his assistant director in there as well. My boss said these words to me: "Sherry, Bobby and I have been talking, and we have decided to give you your promotion six months early. We believe you're ready."

I couldn't believe my ears! I knew God would work it out, but I had no idea He'd work it out so fast! My boss went on to explain the new salary, and it was exactly what I needed to be able to afford an apartment of my own. It all worked out so smoothly and better than I had imagined. This is why I consider this the cornerstone of my faith. I trusted God, and He proved Himself trustworthy, so it established firmly in my soul that God loves me, He cares for my every need, and He will provide whatever I need. Of course, I must do my part, but as long as I am obedient to do my part I can trust Him with His part.

Can you recall a time in your life when you wasted time trying to figure out something about God's plan—either why it was as it was, how He would accomplish it, or maybe even another way it could be done? If so, describe it.

_____

_____

_____

A few years ago while visiting with my college roommate and precious friend, Sherry Blankenship, who serves as a hospital chaplain, I asked her what she said to someone who was at the point of death and there was no time for a presentation of the Gospel. She said she would say to them to pray simply, "I trust You, Jesus, I trust You, Jesus," saying it over and over again. I loved that story and I began to make that prayer a part of my interaction with God anytime I face difficulty and need His supernatural strength and direction. It serves as my acknowledgement of God's power and affirmation of my trust in Him.

Life is full of difficulties, and Christians are not exempt from them. There are some difficulties we can avoid when we live lives of obedience to God, but there are others that we can't avoid. However, these can become opportunities to be a display of God's glory and His character. To see a child of God going through difficulty with supernatural grace and peace is inspirational. It says to the world, "God is real in that person's life." This should give others hope that God can be real to them, as well.

We all have opportunities to reveal God even in the small difficulties of life, and we can know that if we're faithful in the small difficulties, we can be faithful in the big ones. **When we face any difficulty, our goal should be to reveal and glorify God. This means that others know that what appears in us as goodness is not really us, but instead God working in us.** Then through that, God is glorified because His power is seen.

First Peter 1:6–7 explains this as follows: "⁶In this you rejoice, though now for a little while, if necessary, you have been grieved by various trials, ⁷so that the tested genuineness of your faith—more precious than gold that perishes though it is tested by fire—may be found to result in praise and glory and honor at the revelation of Jesus Christ."

On one more personal note, I must add that when I face difficulty and turn to God, I also turn to various passages from His Word. My favorite passage is what I call my life passage, which is Hebrews 12:1–2. It reads as follows: "Therefore, since we are surrounded by so great a cloud of witnesses, let us also lay aside every weight, and sin which clings so closely, and let us run with endurance the race that is set before us, ² looking to Jesus, the founder and perfecter of our faith, who for the joy that was set before him endured the cross, despising the shame, and is seated at the right hand of the throne of God."

Every time that I face difficulty and look to this passage for the strength and courage I need, God shows me a fresh application of some part of this passage. One distinct experience was when I was going through a trial and the words *for the joy* just leapt off the page at me. God showed me very clearly that I could get through anything if I focused on the fact that Jesus endured the cross "for the joy" set before Him. I imagined the joy and satisfaction that Jesus must have felt when He ascended to the right hand of the throne of God, knowing that His purpose had been fulfilled and because of that, all humanity could have a relationship with God the Father and all who believe would be able to spend eternity with Him in heaven.

Of course, my purpose is not as lofty as Jesus's purpose, but it's the purpose God has for me. As a result of this message God gave me that morning, I determined to press on in the task God had given me because of the joy that I would one day have when the goal had been accomplished because I'd been obedient to His command. To help me keep this goal in the forefront of my mind, I made four bracelets in various colors with the words *for the joy* as a reminder that I do all I do for the joy I will one day have when my purpose has been fulfilled.

Are you facing difficulty right now? If so, give it to God and allow Him to take control of it. If there's something He tells you to do about it, do it. Otherwise, simply trust Him to help you because He really is faithful and He loves you.

Meditate today on these thoughts from 1 Peter 1:6–7: "⁶In this you rejoice, though now for a little while, if necessary, you have been grieved by various trials, ⁷so that the tested genuineness of your faith—more precious than gold that perishes though it is tested by fire—may be found to result in praise and glory and honor at the revelation of Jesus Christ."

Ask God to help you to focus on His plan for you instead of the details and trials surrounding it and to help you to reveal His glory in all that you do. Also, thank Him for sending His Son so that through Him you can handle the difficulties of this life.

Notes

Day Seven—God With Us

²²All this took place to fulfill what the Lord had spoken by the prophet: ²³"Behold, the virgin shall conceive and bear a son, and they shall call his name Immanuel (which means, God with us)."
—Matthew 1:22–23

Immanuel—God with us! Think about what that means. For us who have a relationship with God through Jesus, it means that the spirit of the living God lives within us! He doesn't just walk beside us; He is *with* us in everything we do, He knows our every thought, He empowers us to live the life He wants us to live, and He guides us in every step we take if we allow Him that freedom. Doing that requires the surrender of our will to His. This is a very big deal that I'm afraid we take way too lightly.

Jesus, however, knew and understood what it meant. In John 8:28–29, He said, "When you have lifted up the Son of Man, then you will know that I am he, and that I do nothing on my own authority, but speak just as the Father taught me. ²⁹And he who sent me is with me. He has not left me alone, for I always do the things that are pleasing to him."

Consider these words again: "I do nothing on my own authority, but speak just as the Father taught me. And he who sent me is with me. He has not left me alone, for I always do the things that are pleasing to him." Even Jesus did nothing on His own, so why would we try to live life on our own or make decisions on our own? Before

Jesus was crucified, He said this to His disciples, as recorded in John 14:15–16, "¹⁵If you love me, you will keep my commandments. ¹⁶And I will ask the Father, and he will give you another Helper, to be with you forever…" We know this Helper as the Holy Spirit of God who lives in the heart of every believer. We who have a relationship with Jesus have the power of the Spirit of our heavenly Father living within us to empower us to live life God's way.

In 1 Thessalonians 3:13, we see the ultimate fulfillment of God with us. Paul's words recorded here are "so that he may establish your hearts blameless in holiness before our God and Father, at the coming of our Lord Jesus with all his saints." We can only be holy because He is with us. His presence allows and enables that. Think about God's glorious plan when He created the universe and all humanity. In the garden of Eden, Adam and Eve enjoyed fellowship with God until they sinned and that fellowship was broken and they were cast out of the garden. From that point until Jesus's crucifixion, sacrifices were offered to cover the sins of the people, but finally the ultimate sacrifice was given *for* humanity by God Himself—His precious Son, Jesus, whose very name means "God with us." It is God's way of abiding with us in a very real way until we can once again be in His presence as Adam and Eve were, but in a glorified body. Jesus's being with us makes us holy in God's eyes.

What does it mean to you that God is with you?

_____

_____

My favorite Christmas decorations are the lights—lights on the trees, lights outlining buildings, lights on garland, lights hung anywhere as a symbol of the celebration of Christmas. I think the reason I enjoy them so much is that to me they symbolize Jesus as the light of the world and the light that His presence brings to our lives. He said, as recorded in John 8:12, "I am the light of the world. Whoever follows me will not walk in darkness, but will have the light of life." First John 1:7 says, "But if we walk in the light, as he is in the light, we have fellowship with one another, and the blood of Jesus his Son cleanses us from all sin."

The Holy Spirit lives in us to light our way to fellowship with the Father and other Christians, as well as to be God's light to a lost and dying world. He shines light on our sins so that we see them as what they are. Then He leads us in repentance if we are willing. He also shines light on the way we should go when we are faced with decisions. Also, God's light is reflected through the life of every believer who is surrendered to the will of God. We've all heard people say that some Christians have a glow about them; that glow is the light of Jesus being reflected through them, hopefully all of us if we live life fully trusting God. Jesus promised that we will never walk in darkness but will have the light of life. No darkness, but the light of life! Do we reflect that light? Do we tell people where it comes from?

Give examples of how you reflect God's light and how you make others know it comes from Him.

_____

_____

_____

Jesus said, as recorded in Matthew 5:14–16, "[14]You are the light of the world. A city set on a hill cannot be hidden. [15]Nor do people light a lamp and put it under a basket, but on a stand, and it gives light to all in the house. [16]In the same way, let your light shine before others, so that they may see your good works and give glory to your Father who is in heaven." So on one occasion Jesus says, "I am the light of the world," and then on another, He says to His followers, "You are the light of the world." This is the heart of Jesus, the one who was called Immanuel—"God with us." He came so that we might have life and have it more abundantly (John 10:10) and the way He did that was by teaching the ways of God, sacrificing His life for the sins of humanity, then sending His Holy Spirit to indwell the heart of every believer so that God is revealed and glorified. **That's the heart of the Gospel—Jesus is the light of the world and we, as His followers, possess that same light through His Holy Spirit so that we can reflect Him to everyone we're around.**

When we think about what "God with us" means to us on a daily basis, we can feel comforted and reassured because we know that God is not just with us as an impartial and helpless bystander. He loves us—He proved that by sending His Son to die on the cross for us—and He, through the power of His Holy Spirit, empowers us to do the things He wants us to do. He's literally with us all the time; He knows our thoughts and our hearts, as well as our actions. His being with us all the time doesn't mean He's going to force His will and His character on us. We have the freedom to choose His enabling.

On a personal note, I must share an example of a time I knew that God was with me and I needed to pay attention. We lived in Gainesville, Georgia, and one afternoon I stopped at a gas station to fill up my car. As I was standing by the pump while the gas was dispensing, I noticed a lady drive up on the other side of the pump. She stopped across from me, and I felt God nudging me to pay attention to her. She kept looking down, and I thought she was probably looking for her cash or credit card. I watched her, assuming that maybe she didn't have her card or money for gas and that God wanted me to buy her gas. I was prepared to ask her if I could fill up her tank.

She finally looked up and saw me looking at her. I smiled at her to let her know I was there to help and spoke to her as she opened her door. She immediately lit up with a huge smile and said, "I own a business, and someone was really rude to me a while ago and I was just sitting here in my car praying and asking God to somehow encourage me. Then I looked up and saw your great big smile! I knew He had answered my prayer!" We talked about how wonderful it is that God uses His children to help each other. I left that encounter with a fresh reminder that God really is with us all the time, even when we're filling up our cars at the service station, and I also noted that so many people just need a smile.

How aware are you all through every day of the Holy Spirit's presence in your life? As Christians, we should be continually aware of how our thoughts and attitudes line up with God's will and His character. If you sense a straying away from what those should be, pray a simple prayer of "Help me, Jesus" to get you back on track. This is also a helpful prayer when you feel overwhelmed and know you can't do what God wants you to do on your own. We should remind ourselves that His Spirit lives in us for such a time as this to empower us to do God's will.

What difference does the fact that God is with you make in your everyday life? Give examples of times when you were particularly aware of His presence.

_____

_____

_____

One huge benefit of the fact that God is with us is the value He adds to our lives. Consider that you owned a stock that was valued at a relatively low price. Then one day the company was bought by a man who was considered the wisest and most successful man in the financial world. Imagine the increase this stock would experience. Now think about the fact that the God of the universe, if you're His child, lives in you and longs to lead you every single step of your life. This realization should leave absolutely no room for insecurity or a low self-esteem. He adds incredible value to your life.

Psalm 23 gives a beautiful picture of what it means to have God with us. It would be a good idea to read that passage as you conclude today's study.

Meditate today on Matthew 1:23: "Behold, the virgin shall conceive and bear a son, and they shall call his name Immanuel (which means, God with us)." Throughout the day, ask God to make you more aware than ever before of His presence with you and thank Him for sending His Son to be born in the flesh and literally walk with you so that so that you can experience the ultimate reality of being with Him throughout eternity.

Notes

Day Eight—Authority

In those days a decree went out from Caesar
Augustus that all the world should be registered.
²This was the first registration when Quirinius was
governor of Syria. ³And all went to be registered,
each to his own town. ⁴And Joseph also went up
from Galilee, from the town of Nazareth, to Judea,
to the city of David, which is called Bethlehem,
because he was of the house and lineage of David,
⁵to be registered with Mary, his betrothed, who was
with child.

—Luke 2:1–5

Try to put yourself in Mary and Joseph's shoes. Imagine how
they must have agonized over the timing of this census and
the necessity to travel at least a three days' journey when Mary was
about to have the baby Jesus. All the questions that we might have
asked may have gone through their minds as they looked at Caesar
Augustus as the one in authority, the one responsible for their
having to travel to Bethlehem. Or maybe they did realize that it
had been prophesied in scripture that the Messiah would be born
in Bethlehem. Nevertheless, it was a difficult time for them.

Now put yourself in Caesar Augustus' shoes. Whether this idea
for a census came from him or from someone under him, he had
the authority to make it happen—or did he? In reality, God had the
plan all along, and He orchestrated all the events to make it happen

His way and in His time. God was in control then just as He is today. He is the ultimate authority.

Think about people who have authority over you. Hopefully, you see God as the ultimate authority that He is, but who else has authority over you?

Romans 13:1–6 says,

> [1]Let every person be subject to the governing authorities. For there is no authority except from God, and those that exist have been instituted by God. [2]Therefore whoever resists the authorities resists what God has appointed, and those who resist will incur judgment. [3]For rulers are not a terror to good conduct, but to bad. Would you have no fear of the one who is in authority? Then do what is good, and you will receive his approval, [4]for he is God's servant for your good. But if you do wrong, be afraid, for he does not bear the sword in vain. For he is the servant of God, an avenger who carries out God's wrath on the wrongdoer. [5]Therefore one must be in subjection, not only to avoid God's wrath but also for the sake of conscience. [6]For because of this you also pay taxes, for the authorities are ministers of God, attending to this very thing.

We see here that God established governing authorities to bring about order in the world and to punish those who do wrong. We Christians should hold our authorities in high esteem and show respect for them. Sure, there are those in authority who usurp their authority, and we will discuss that later, but first, we should consider how we should respect anyone in authority over us.

Christians should be the most loving, obedient, respectful, and hardworking people the world knows, and should capture the attention of our government authorities and employers as such. As employees, we should respect our employers and do the job given us to the very best of our abilities. Then although a man or woman may be over us as our boss, we should recognize that God is the giver of authority and He is ultimately in control of the job we have and the pay we receive. He can and will work in the hearts of those in authority to accomplish His will. When we don't get a job, raise, or promotion, we can rest in the assurance that God's in control.

Life can be so much less stressful if we simply trust God with every aspect of it and realize that even though others may be "over" us, God is ultimately in control of all that happens to us. Therefore, we need to abandon the thought that those we see as being in authority over us are really in control of all that happens to us. For example, if a job or promotion is not received, don't blame the person over you who seemingly made the decision. If God had wanted you to have the job or promotion, He could have worked through the person in "authority" to bring that about.

I learned this principle of God's control years ago. I went through a period of feeling bitter about what I viewed as inequities in many situations surrounding Tommy's job. One morning as I agonized over this in my prayer time, God spoke to me inaudibly, but very clearly, and said something like this: "Do you really think Tommy's boss is in control of where he works and how much he makes? He is not. I AM."

All of a sudden, my eyes were opened, and my heart was changed from an attitude of whining to one of gratitude. My prayer suddenly became, "Thank you, Lord, for putting us where we are and for the gracious salary you have blessed us with." This was such a freeing experience because I no longer felt that we were at the mercy of various bosses in the corporate world. I could rest in the assurance that God was in control of every part of our lives.

This same mindset should carry over into every aspect of our lives that involves someone in authority, even our churches and civic organizations. We should always trust God to give us the opportunities to be used by Him and never allow our flesh to intervene and manipulate situations that give us leadership out of self-promotion. Through the years, we've seen choir members leave a church because they didn't get to sing the solos they wanted to sing and others change churches because they didn't get to teach or have other responsibilities they thought they should have. This is so sad because if we simply trust God to open the doors for us to serve Him in ways that He wills, we will have those opportunities to do what He calls us to do, and we'll know that they've come from Him.

It takes humility to wait on Him and trust Him, but the reward is great! The best antidote for self-promotion is to remember that only those acts done for God and His glory will stand the test of fire. Those works done for any other reason will one day be burned. First Corinthians 3:15 says, "If anyone's work is burned up, he will suffer loss, though he himself will be saved, but only as through fire."

Next, let's consider what to do when authorities over us act in ways that are not in line with God's Word. Some governmental and private authorities have been allowed to require or prohibit activities that would require Christians to go against their adherence to God's Word and, therefore, His will for them. Acts 4:1–4 and 18–21 tell a story that illustrates this. In this passage we read,

> [1]And as they were speaking to the people, the priests and the captain of the temple and the Sadducees came upon them, [2] greatly annoyed because they were teaching the people and proclaiming in Jesus the resurrection from the dead. [3] And they arrested them and put them in custody until the next day, for it was already evening. [4]But many of those who had heard the word believed, and the number of the men came to about five thousand … [18]So they

called them and charged them not to speak or teach at all in the name of Jesus. [19] But Peter and John answered them, "Whether it is right in the sight of God to listen to you rather than to God, you must judge, [20] for we cannot but speak of what we have seen and heard." [21] And when they had further threatened them, they let them go, finding no way to punish them, because of the people, for all were praising God for what had happened.

According to verse 2, the government leaders were annoyed because the apostles were teaching about the resurrection of Jesus. The remarks of Peter and John made them feel uncomfortable. Does that sound familiar? So they put them in jail overnight and then questioned them the next day. Verse 18 records the order for Peter and John not to speak or teach at all in the name of Jesus. Write Peter and John's response in your own words.

_____

_____

Do you think Peter and John's response would have been different if this order had come from their boss in the workplace today? Do you think their response is the appropriate response from similar pressure today?

_____

One other thing to note is that the Christian community may have supported each other in that day possibly more than we do today. According to verse 21, why could the authorities not decide how to punish Peter and John?

_____

Matthew 28:18–20 says, "[18] And Jesus came and said to them, 'All authority in heaven and on earth has been given to me. [19] Go therefore and make disciples of all nations, baptizing them in the name of the Father and of the Son and of the Holy Spirit, [20] teaching them to observe all that I have commanded you. And behold, I am with you always, to the end of the age.'" So who has authority in heaven and on earth? _____ Let's apply this to our lives today.

Meditate today on this phrase from Matthew 28:18–20: "All authority in heaven and on earth has been given to me." Throughout the day, ask God to help you acknowledge Him as your supreme authority and to help you trust Him to control what He wants you to do and to give you the courage to not forsake Him and His commands when His authority is challenged. Also, thank God for sending His Son to be born in the flesh so that you can trust in His authority over your life.

Notes

DAY NINE—NO ROOM

> [7]And she gave birth to her firstborn son and wrapped him in swaddling cloths and laid him in a manger, because there was no place for them in the inn.
>
> —Luke 2:7

The events surrounding Jesus's birth are indicative of the way God's mind differs from ours. Our mindset would have probably been like this: God knew that Mary and Joseph would be in Bethlehem for the census; therefore, He would have arranged for the best room in the inn to be miraculously available when they arrived. After all, He wanted only the best for His Son. We know, however, that did not happen. Upon Mary and Joseph's arrival, there was no room for them—and she was about to deliver the promised Messiah. How absurd that could seem to us if we only looked at it from our standpoints instead of God's. From His angle, though, it was an appropriate way to demonstrate the humility that Jesus would spend His earthly life teaching about and modeling.

Let's look at what the two words *no room* can mean to us today. Jesus isn't looking for an inn today, but He's looking for hearts in which He can live. And He's too often finding the same no-room message. Could it be that people, even Christians, have no time for Jesus because they don't really know who He is, just as the innkeeper did not realize who these people were?

Let's look at exactly who Jesus, God incarnate, really is. The

Bible is full of descriptions of God, but we will pull out only a few. Following each scripture, use one or two words to describe who the passage says that God is.

"Before the mountains were brought forth, or ever you had formed the earth and the world, from everlasting to everlasting you are God" (Psalm 90:2) _____

"In the beginning, God created the heavens and the earth" (Genesis 1:1) _____

"My help comes from the LORD, who made heaven and earth" (Psalm 121:2) _____

"Because he holds fast to me in love, I will deliver him; I will protect him, because he knows my name" (Psalm 91:14). _____

"Know therefore that the LORD your God is God, the faithful God who keeps covenant and steadfast love with those who love him and keep his commandments, to a thousand generations" (Deuteronomy 7:9). _____

"To the Lord our God belong mercy and forgiveness, for we have rebelled against him" (Daniel 9:9). _____

"There is none holy like the LORD: for there is none besides you; there is no rock like our God" (1 Samuel 2:2). _____

"For God so loved the world, that he gave his only Son, that whoever believes in him should not perish but have eternal life" (John 3:16). _____

"I am the good shepherd. I know my own and my own know me" (John 10:14)

_____

God is all these things and much more. How, then, can we not have room for Him in our hearts and lives? If the innkeeper had just realized who Mary and Joseph were and who this baby was, he would have had others move out to make room for the Messiah. In the same way, we may have other people or things taking the place in our heart that belongs to God.

The first "other" could be ourselves, in the form of self-centeredness. Another "other" could be our mate. Others could be our children, friends, and so on. Others could also include material things or jobs. Spend a few minutes examining your heart for who or what could be taking the place that God wants and deserves in your heart. List people or things that come to mind.

_____

_____

The point of the study today is that we must not only make room for God in our lives, but He must *be* our lives. Let's look at some specific ways we can tell if He has His proper place in our hearts.

1. Because our heart's affection and devotion must be on Him before anyone else, we will spend the time with Him that is necessary to build a love relationship that will supersede all our other relationships. It will be the relationship that governs everything we do.
2. We will allow Him to control our to-do list. He determines what's really important and what is not, so we will pray over

our schedule and ask Him to help us do the things that He wants us to do. As we go through each day, we will be so aware of His presence that we allow Him to interrupt or change our plans as He presents unexpected opportunities to minister to others.

3. We will pray about and evaluate opportunities for involvement as they arise to determine whether God is directing us to do them. We will make sure that we do not commit to activities, even in the church, that are not God's will for us, realizing that busyness is a leading cause of having no room for God.

4. The way we handle situations will be guided by what is acceptable and pleasing to God.

5. We will be obedient to His every command.

If we Christians get a grasp of who God really is, then we will live in such a way that our lives will reveal Him to non-Christians, and they will be led to a saving knowledge of Him as well.

Do you have room for God in your heart and life? If not, surrender your will right now to do whatever it takes to make room for Him—not just among all your other priorities, but so that He *is* your priority and everything else lines up with His will.

Meditate today on Deuteronomy 6:5: "You shall love the LORD your God with all your heart and with all your soul and with all your might." Throughout the day, ask God to help you surrender your whole heart to Him and to reveal to you if at any point you allow other people or things to take the place in your heart that belongs to Him.

Notes

Day Ten—The Most Precious Gift

> And she gave birth to her firstborn son and wrapped
> him in swaddling cloths and laid him in a manger,
> because there was no place for them in the inn.
>
> —Luke 2:7

The time had finally come for the Messiah to be born. This event had been prophesied through the ages, and it had finally come to pass. Yet it could have seemed so insignificant—a common couple finding shelter in a stable. Visualize in your mind for a few moments what it must have been like in that stable. Smell the scent of the animals and the musty odor of the hay. Hear the sounds of the animals; they are oblivious to what has just happened.

But Mary and Joseph are ecstatic over their firstborn son, the Messiah promised by the angel. Do you think Mary may have wondered what He would look like? Would He look different from any other baby? They must have been in awe at really being able to look into the eyes of God's Son as their precious baby boy. Think of the wonder they must have felt. Describe the emotions you can imagine they felt.

_____

_____

Mary and Joseph could possibly have looked into the eyes of Jesus and asked themselves, "What do we do with You now—the promised Messiah? How do we care for the child of the God of the universe?" This prompts me to ask myself a similar question: "What do I do with the gift of Jesus?"

I think about how every year we get some Christmas presents that go on a shelf in the closet and never get used. Then we get some that we use occasionally, and we get others that we love and use all the time. Which of these categories does Jesus fit in? Have you put Him on a shelf to never use, have you put Him where you can get to Him when you need Him in an emergency, or have you taken Him as the most precious gift ever received and continually allowed Him full rein over your heart?

Jesus doesn't want to be tucked away in a corner of your heart only to be used in emergencies. He wants to be the guiding force of your life. He wants to be the most precious gift you will ever receive because He is! What, then, do we do with this precious gift? List some things that you have done with the gift of Jesus.

_____

_____

_____

_____

Here are some ideas:

First, you accept Jesus as your personal Savior, which is the purpose for which He was born. Have you accepted Jesus's death and resurrection as payment for your sins and given your life to Him? _____ If not, why? _____

_____

Second, you spend time with Him every day, allowing Him to fill you with His power and presence so that you're able to handle whatever comes your way. Do you have daily Bible study and prayer time, quiet times with God? _____ If so, consider the quality of these times and ask God to show you ways to make them more meaningful and impactful on your life. If you don't, would you consider starting this practice and challenging yourself to study the Bible daily, allowing God to apply it to your heart and life so that you live in a way that's consistent with its teachings? _____

_____

Third, you go about your day doing the things that you know God wants you to do. This includes such activities as working a job to provide for your family, cleaning your house, and preparing meals to meet the needs of your family, and various other activities that you know He wants you to do. You do these activities to the very best of your ability because you know that He requires the best of you and He can empower you to give your best. How would you rate your consistency in doing the things you know God wants you to do to the best of the ability He gives you?

_____ all the time _____ frequently _____ occasionally _____ never

Fourth, as you go about these activities, you share Him with others so that they can know, too, the joy of this precious gift. It's incredible to think that many people around us don't even know about the most precious gift ever given to mankind. They may know His name and a few facts about Him, but they may not have a clue as to who He really is and that He wants a personal relationship with them. What can you do to be more focused on sharing the Gospel of Jesus with others?

_____

Fifth, you help others in need around you, realizing that you are God's hands to them. A vital way that God ministers to the needy is by the hands of His children. We must be sensitive to His voice and obedient to do what He asks us to do. Evaluate your servant spirit. Do you need to improve in your ability to set your desires aside to serve others? _____

_____

Sixth, you trust Jesus with everything and allow Him to fill your heart with His love, joy and peace so that you're able to reflect Him more clearly to others.

Considering the six steps discussed, look back at each one and write your plan to be more effective and intentional in each area so that you can make the impact on the world that God desires of you. You cannot do it on your own, but if you allow God to pour into you His words, wisdom, and power, He will accomplish things through you that you would never have imagined.

1. _____
2. _____
3. _____
4. _____
5. _____
6. _____

Consider what you will do with the gift of Jesus. Which category of gifts will He be in—the one that gets put on the shelf and never used, the one that is used occasionally, or the one that is taken to heart as the most precious possession you have? He loves you so much that He gave up the glory of heaven to come and live on this earth and give His life for you. What will be your response to Him?

Meditate today on Luke 2:7: "And she gave birth to her firstborn son and wrapped him in swaddling cloths and laid him in a manger, because there was no place for them in the inn." Throughout the day, focus on the impact this gift of Jesus has had and can have on your life. Ask God to help you give Him the proper love and obedience in response to this precious gift. Thank Him for this gift of Jesus, the most precious gift ever given to mankind.

Notes

Day Eleven—A Humble Beginning

And she gave birth to her firstborn son and wrapped
him in swaddling cloths and laid him in a manger,
because there was no place for them in the inn.
—Luke 2:7

As mentioned two days ago, God could have made available to
Mary and Joseph the finest accommodations that Bethlehem
had to offer. However, not only was the best room not available,
no room at all was available, thus causing Mary and Joseph to seek
shelter in the humblest of surroundings: a stable. What a humble
start to such an important life—the most important person to
ever walk the earth! **Humility would play an important role in
Jesus's ministry as He set the example for all of mankind. In
fact, it's the very foundation of our relationship with God, for
we cannot approach God without humbling ourselves before
Him in realization of who He is and who we are.** It's also the
key to lasting and thriving relationships with others. Therefore,
God chose the humblest of settings for the birth of Jesus. At that
time, Mary and Joseph may not have understood the "why" of it
all, but because of the character we've already seen in them, they
probably accepted it in the same humility that Jesus would later
teach about.

Because humility played such an important role in the birth
of Jesus, I think it would be helpful for us to look at what it really
means and how we can apply it to our lives.

James 4:10 says, "Humble yourselves before the Lord, and he will exalt you." The Greek word used here for the word *humble* is *tapeinoo*, which means "to humble or lower oneself, to be brought low, in need." To humble ourselves, then, means to intentionally and willingly submit to the authority of another, and it denotes a mindset of self-denial. To humble ourselves before God involves a conscious act of lowering ourselves and submitting to His authority, realizing our need for Him, and it's driven by seeing who God is and our inability to measure up on our own. Our focus here is on God, so we see Him as the plumb line, or the standard. If we compare ourselves to others, we can always find someone else who makes us feel pretty good about ourselves. However, our only true assessment comes from a look at ourselves compared to God. From that perspective, we can see ourselves first as sinners, then as forgiven, and finally as blessed. At that point, we can see God as the source of all that is good in us. It's then, when we humble ourselves before God, that He lifts us up. We are then useful to Him because He can fill us with His power after we have emptied ourselves of self.

Philippians 2:5–11 says,

> [5] Have this mind among yourselves, which is yours in Christ Jesus, [6] who, though he was in the form of God, did not count equality with God a thing to be grasped, [7] but emptied himself, by taking the form of a servant, being born in the likeness of men. [8] And being found in human form, he humbled himself by becoming obedient to the point of death, even death on a cross. [9] Therefore God has highly exalted him and bestowed on him the name that is above every name, [10] so that at the name of Jesus every knee should bow, in heaven and on earth and under the earth, [11] and every tongue confess that Jesus Christ is Lord, to the glory of God the Father.

Verse 7 gives a great description of what humility is all about. Write it in your own words.

_____

_____

My good friend, Ann McGraw, once told me that she'd heard a preacher say that the test of whether you're a servant is how you respond when you're treated like one. Think about it. What's your response when someone treats you like a servant?

_____

_____

Verse 7 says that Jesus "emptied himself, by taking the form of a servant." The word *taking* tells us that it was a conscious choice that He made. We have the same choice. Verse 8 says that Jesus "humbled himself by becoming obedient." The desire to be obedient causes us to surrender ourselves to God. What is described in verses 10 and 11?

_____

_____

Jesus is right now seated on His throne at the right hand of God. He first humbled Himself by leaving heaven's glory to be born in a stable manger. Then He was lifted up on the cross so that we could be lifted up to Him. Then He ascended to heaven for the fulfillment of His being lifted up. If we have accepted His sacrifice as payment for our sins, we can also be lifted up to live with Him in heaven throughout eternity. So, you see, God absolutely wants the very best for His children. It is the best that comes from humbling ourselves first and submitting to His authority in our lives, being obedient to His commands.

The way that humility is manifested in us is our willingness to put others' needs and desires above our own. Self-centeredness is an inborn human trait that must be relinquished in order for us to be servants. Jesus's command about it is recorded in Matthew 16:24: "If anyone would come after me, let him deny himself and take up his cross and follow me." This denying of self is the casting away of self-centeredness, our own desires, and placing our focus on what God desires of us. He desires that we take on His character so that we can reveal His glory to others around us. Be very intentional in your desire to maintain a servant attitude as you relate to God and others. Remember that it is not a natural attitude, but one that only God can help you establish. Ask Him to empty you of yourself and replace your sinfulness with His character. An important principle to note here is that this is a daily thing; it is not something that can be done once and for all.

Let's look at what humility looks like when it is displayed in people today. Here are some examples of where it's seen:

- the person who is willing to sincerely say, "I'm sorry. I was wrong."
- the person who does not get indignant when someone cuts in front of him in line or in traffic
- the person who lovingly yields his own desires to meet the needs of others
- the person who loves the person who has wronged him and does not hold a grudge
- the person who willingly gives up the best seat in the house for another person
- the person who gives a gracious tip to the server who has given poor service because he realizes how merciful God has been to him
- the person who is willing to consider another person's opinion and responds lovingly in acceptance or rejection of their opinion
- the person who takes a risk at restoring a broken relationship and does it lovingly

- the person who takes a stand for Biblical truth without attacking or demeaning another person
- the person who does not fear persecution, but graciously shares the Gospel with others so they, too, can know Jesus
- the person who sees all others as the people loved by God that they are
- the person who loves others unconditionally

Whatever difficulty you may be going through, humble yourself before God and accept His authority over your life. Just as it was God's will for Jesus to be born in a stable, it may be God's will for you to be humbled by enduring hardship at times so that He can lift you up. Sometimes I believe He withholds blessings so that we're prepared for even greater blessings later on and so that we learn to look to Him to meet our needs.

Meditate today on this part of Philippians 2:8: "He humbled himself by becoming obedient to the point of death, even death on a cross." Throughout the day, ask God to help you get a grasp of what humility really means and to help you take on the nature of a servant in total obedience to God so that you're able to reveal God's glory and His nature in everything you do. Also, thank God for sending His Son in the manner that He did as a demonstration of true humility.

Notes

Day Twelve—A Heavenly Celebration

For to us a child is born, to us a son is given; and
the government shall be upon his shoulder, and his
name shall be called Wonderful Counselor, Mighty
God, Everlasting Father, Prince of Peace.

—Isaiah 9:6

Before we move along with the events surrounding the birth of
Jesus, it would be good to dwell on the magnificence of what
has just happened. Isaiah had prophesied about it around seven
hundred years before it actually came to pass. This truly was the
promised Messiah who would save people from the penalty of their
sins and impact the world in a way that no other person has ever
done. Think for a moment about the angels in heaven who knew
what was happening and the purpose of it all. This was probably
the most spectacular event they had ever witnessed.

During the first Christmas season after my daddy died, God
led me to celebrate that season as my daddy's first Christmas in
heaven instead of my first Christmas without him. That gave me the
ability to, as much as possible, see Christmas through his eyes and,
therefore, enjoy a fresh perspective of Christmas and the celebration
of it as I had never before known.

As that Christmas approached, I knew that it would be a
difficult season, but I also knew that my daddy was with God

because he had a relationship with Jesus Christ. Because of this and because of the positive attitude he had always manifested, I knew that he would want me to find a positive way of approaching the season. As I agonized with God over how that would happen, He led me to study the Christmas story in a much deeper way than I had ever before done. One of the first mornings I did this, I began to wonder what it would be like if those in heaven celebrated Christmas.

Now I realize this is a strange question because every day in heaven is a celebration with God on His throne, Jesus at His right hand, and all the magnificence there. But just for the sake of imagining how they would celebrate what Jesus did for mankind, I envisioned God summoning the heavenly choir and having them sing praises to Jesus. Just picture what that would be like. The heavenly choir is majestically singing praises to Jesus more beautifully than we have ever heard, accompanied by heavenly instruments that make this a truly spectacular event. Everyone there is around the throne praising Jesus with uplifted hands and bowed knees, knowing that His coming to earth as a baby that Christmas is the reason they are there.

I knew that my daddy was in that group surrounding the throne and being part of the celebration for the first time. I could imagine the joy that he must have, and I would not have taken that joy away from him even if I had been able to bring him back. I next imagined walking up to him and asking him what he wanted for Christmas, since on earth a major way that we celebrate Christmas is by giving presents to those we love. I didn't want to ignore him just because he was no longer here physically. I knew he would say to me something like this: "Just tell everyone you know what Jesus did for them and ask them to accept His sacrifice as payment for their sins because they don't want to miss this!" And he would probably add something along these lines: "Spend your time focusing on what's important to God instead of all the trivialities that can absorb your mind and your time."

This changed my perspective of the way we celebrate Christmas. It is too much about us and too little about Jesus. This experience allowed me to celebrate my daddy's first Christmas in heaven instead of being overwhelmed with the sadness of our being without him, and it also caused me to see Christmas through different eyes. My idea of what that heavenly celebration would be like stayed in the forefront of my mind throughout that Christmas season and has continued to be one of my primary focuses every Christmas since then.

For my daddy's Christmas present that year, I wrote a letter to a man to whom he had witnessed several times. Because my daddy had shared with me some of what he had said to his friend, I was able to remind him of those things, and I asked him to reconsider his rejection of Jesus and accept Him as his personal Savior. Daddy had taught a Sunday school class of men in their forties and fifties, and he had a special ministry of wanting to reach men with the Gospel. I have no doubt that he still has that desire, and even more so now that he's experiencing heaven! And I also have no doubt that he would tell me that same message today—to reach everyone I can with the Gospel because they do *not* want to miss heaven.

What about you? Do you have a loved one who you believe is in heaven and will also be able to celebrate this Christmas season in the presence of Jesus and all His glory? If so, imagine for a moment that you could walk up to him or her in the middle of the celebration and ask what you could do for him or her as a special Christmas present. Write the name of the loved one and state what you believe that person would want you to do for his or her Christmas present this season.

Now imagine you're in that crowd celebrating Jesus. What do you think you'll wish you'd done differently in this life?

_____

_____

What things or activities would have less importance to you and what things or activities would have more importance to you? Write your thoughts.

_____

_____

_____

You probably included the fact that you will wish you'd told more people about Jesus so they could be there with you. I believe that could be the single most common regret when we get to heaven. Consider what you can do about this now while you still have the chance. If you're a believer, list some names of unbelievers with whom you would like to share the Gospel. Then develop your plan to do it.

_____

_____

_____

Last year, I had a tract printed that I had written to give people with whom I have contact but not enough time to really share all I would like to say to them. I wanted to give people a tract in my own words, and I usually say when I give it to them that it's what I would love to share with them about Jesus if we had ten minutes over coffee. I mention that Jesus is the key to the abundant life and to eternal life in heaven. Then I tell them my phone number is on the back if they would like to call me to have coffee and discuss how they can really know Jesus. I give it to cashiers, servers, and anyone else I have brief contact with. I also give it to people I do have time to share the Gospel with but want them to have something that they can read later to help them understand what I said.

Sharing Jesus with others is the best way we can celebrate Him and what He did for us. It is our way of obeying His command given to us, His followers, in the Great Commission recorded in Matthew 28:19–20: "Go therefore and make disciples of all nations, baptizing them in the name of the Father and of the Son and of the Holy Spirit, teaching them to observe all that I have commanded you. And behold, I am with you always, to the end of the age." Consider adopting the phrase "live missionally" as your celebration of who Jesus is and who you are as His follower. Remember, too, that you must be prepared to share Him through living a life consistent with His teachings.

Meditate today on these words from Isaiah 9:6a: "For to us a child is born, to us a son is given." Focus on the heavenly celebration that surrounded the birth of Jesus and ask God to fill you with a sense of celebration through His Holy Spirit so that you can experience His Gift of Jesus at a deeper level than ever before.

Notes

Day Thirteen—The Fullness of Jesus

For to us a child is born, to us a son is given; and the government shall be upon his shoulder, and his name shall be called Wonderful Counselor, Mighty God, Everlasting Father, Prince of Peace.

—Isaiah 9:6

Yesterday, we focused on the celebration of the birth of Jesus and the glorious gift that He is. Today we'll look at the second half of this verse and consider what these titles mean to us who believe in Him: Wonderful Counselor, Mighty God, Everlasting Father, Prince of Peace.

There are so many reasons to celebrate Jesus, the main one being the salvation He brought to all who would accept Him. Another reason for celebration is the help He gives us all along our paths as we follow Him. These four descriptions in the verse above sum up everything that Jesus offers when we've accepted His gift of salvation, and they're everything we need to live the life He calls us to live.

Before we consider these names, however, we should establish the fact that Jesus and God are one so you are not confused when scriptures refer to God as all these things, as well. One reason among many we know this fact is seen in the passage above in the message God gave Isaiah. In referring to this child, one title is "Mighty God," so God Himself refers to the two of them as being one. Then during his earthly ministry, Jesus is quoted in John 10:27–30 and 37–38 as saying,

> [27]My sheep hear my voice, and I know them, and they follow me. [28]I give them eternal life, and they will never perish, and no one will snatch them out of my hand. [29]My Father, who has given them to me, is greater than all, and no one is able to snatch them out of the Father's hand. [30]*I and the Father are one* … [37]If I am not doing the works of my Father, then do not believe me, [38]but if I do them, even though you do not believe me, believe the works, that you may know and understand that *the Father is in me and I am in the Father.* (Emphasis added)

Jesus and God are two parts of the Trinity, and the third is the Holy Spirit (the Spirit of God who lives inside of every believer). They're all one but serve three different roles. Now let's dive into the four titles given to Jesus from our focus passage for today.

As our *Wonderful Counselor,* Jesus leads us on the right and glorious path He has planned for each one of us. Think about the fact that you have your own personal counselor who is available to you 24/7, and not only will He listen to you, but also He has the power to work out every detail of your life. In addition, He loves you more than any other person in the world.

When you face a problem, to whom do you turn first?

If we're aligned with God, we will seek Him first when we have a problem or a decision to make. In order to habitually do that, we must know Him, really know Him in a way that we understand when He speaks to us. This comes from spending quality time with Him every day, studying His Word and praying to Him, being sure to listen to Him. Anytime we believe Jesus is speaking to us, we need to make sure that what we hear aligns with His Word, because He will never tell us something that doesn't. Intimate fellowship with Jesus gives us knowledge and wisdom to follow Him. As we follow Him, we see the expansive meaning of Him as our Wonderful Counselor. Below is a sampling of these facets:

- For sins, He offers forgiveness and reconciliation.
- For discouragement, He reminds us of His love, restores our confidence and sets our feet on the solid ground for the race He has set before us.
- For pain, He offers the comfort of His loving arms.
- For guidance, He offers direction.
- For confusion, He offers clarity.
- For help, He extends His hand.
- For strength, He provides power and wisdom.

Your request for help may be a simple, "Help me, Jesus," and He'll be there for you. There are many, many Bible verses that describe the help that's offered through God and His Son, Jesus. Below is a sampling of them:

- "If we confess our sins, he is faithful and just to forgive us our sins and to cleanse us from all unrighteousness" (First John 1:9).
- "Behold, God is my helper; the Lord is the upholder of my life" (Psalm 54:4).
- "For he delivers the needy when he calls, the poor and him who has no helper" (Psalm 72:12).
- "The Lord is on my side as my helper; I shall look in triumph on those who hate me" (Psalm 118:7).
- "Your testimonies are my delight; they are my counselors" (Psalm 119:24).
- "So we can confidently say, 'The Lord is my helper; I will not fear; what can man do to me?'" (Hebrews 13:6).
- "Though he fall, he will not be cast headlong, for the Lord upholds his hand" (Psalm 37:24).

Determine in your heart to allow Jesus to be the first one to whom you turn when you need help or encouragement.

Second, Jesus is the *Mighty God* who can conquer any obstacle or difficulty we will ever face. The most powerful superhero in any movie you've ever seen can't hold a candle to the mighty power of God. Think about the fact that He created the universe from nothing. We could go on and on about all the details of how magnificent creation is, but let it suffice to say that only God has the power to perform these mighty acts, and only God can sustain what He has created. Just in the short years of Jesus's ministry, He raised the dead to life, healed the sick, restored sight to the blind, made the lame to walk, turned water into wine, and performed many other miracles. Then throughout the Old Testament we read about God parting the Red Sea, feeding the Israelites with manna from heaven, protecting Daniel and his friends in the lions' den, and so many other miraculous acts.

Do you think you can have any problem that is too difficult for God to handle? One thought that I've reminded myself of when I've faced a problem that seemed unsolvable was, "God raised Jesus from death, so why do I think He can't handle my problem?" If God wants something to happen, He will bring it about. Here is a sampling of verses that speak of His mighty power:

- "The voice of the Lord is powerful; the voice of the Lord is full of majesty" (Psalm 29:4).
- "Summon your power, O God, the power, O God, by which you have worked for us" (Psalm 68:28).
- "Once God has spoken; twice have I heard this: that power belongs to God" (Psalm 62:11).
- "Awesome is God from his sanctuary; the God of Israel— he is the one who gives power and strength to his people. Blessed be God!" (Psalm 68:35).

- "For the Lord your God is God of gods and Lord of lords, the great, the mighty, and the awesome God, who is not partial and takes no bribe" (Deuteronomy 10:17).
- "And God raised the Lord and will also raise us up by his power" (First Corinthians 6:14).

Are you facing a problem right now that seems unsolvable to you? If so, describe it and write a prayer asking God for His help in resolving it. If not, describe a time when you've seen God's power in your life or in those around you.

_____

_____

_____

Determine to daily exercise your faith and understanding of God's mighty power. Most people lose sleep and endure stress simply because of unbelief in the power of God to help them overcome difficulties. Rest in the fact that Jesus is called Mighty God and is able to overcome whatever it is you face.

Third, Jesus is our _Everlasting Father_, and He demonstrated it so clearly when He laid down His life for us. What loving father wouldn't protect his family from the evil one by giving his life for them? Jesus gave His life so that we can be protected and then delivered into eternal life with Him. He is the Everlasting Father who will always love us, will never leave us or forsake us, but will always protect us and keep His loving arms wrapped around us.

We think of our earthly fathers as those who love us, provide for us, protect us, guide us, discipline us, encourage us, stand by us, and perform many other acts for our good. You may not have had a father who did all these things, but if you have a relationship with Jesus, you for sure have a heavenly Father who does all of this and so much more! He loves you more than anyone else, and He longs to fulfill your needs; He longs to hold you and allow you to feel the strength of His power and love. When you feel the need for that wonderful and soothing fatherly love, imagine crawling up in Jesus's lap and allow Him to wrap His arms around you as your loving Father. After all, He really is that.

Here is a sampling of Bible verses concerning Jesus and God as our Father:

- "Just as the Father knows me and I know the Father; and I lay down my life for the sheep" (John 10:15).
- "[7]It is for discipline that you have to endure. God is treating you as sons. For what son is there whom his father does not discipline? [8]If you are left without discipline, in which all have participated, then you are illegitimate children and not sons. [9]Besides this, we have had earthly fathers who disciplined us and we respected them. Shall we not much more be subject to the Father of spirits and live? [10]For they disciplined us for a short time as it seemed best to them, but he disciplines us for our good, that we may share his holiness" (Hebrews 12:7–10).
- "Every good gift and every perfect gift is from above, coming down from the Father of lights, with whom there is no variation or shadow due to change" (James 1:17).

Write your thoughts concerning seeing Jesus as your everlasting Father. Include what difference that makes in your life.

_____

_____

Fourth, Jesus is our *Prince of Peace* to continually assure us of His presence and love. He offers the only true peace and it is not peace with the world, but peace with God. I have learned that peace with God is something that a non-Christian can see in a Christian and will intrigue him or her to know where it comes from. I have a close friend who was a business colleague for about eight years, and after we'd worked together for a few months, she said to me one day, "You have a peace that I don't have. Where does it come from?" This peace is exhibited by handling life with its stresses through our relationship with Jesus and seeing life from God's perspective and Jesus as our Wonderful Counselor, Mighty God and Everlasting Father. Jesus as the Prince of Peace is, then, the end result of the build-up of the other three; we can have peace with God now and through all eternity because He is all of these.

Here is a sampling of this peace that Jesus offers:

- "I have said these things to you, that in me you may have peace. In the world you will have tribulation. But take heart; I have overcome the world" (John 16:33).
- "And the peace of God, which surpasses all understanding, will guard your hearts and your minds in Christ Jesus" (Philippians 4:7).
- "You keep him in perfect peace whose mind is stayed on you, because he trusts in you" (Isaiah 26:3).
- "Peace I leave with you; my peace I give to you. Not as the world gives do I give to you. Let not your hearts be troubled, neither let them be afraid" (John 14:27).

Would you say that most of the time you have this peace that comes only from a relationship with Jesus? If not, considering all that you've studied about Him, what do you need to do in order to have it?

_____

_____

Seek this peace that is yours for the taking if you belong to Jesus. Life is so much better when we can keep our hearts and minds clear of internal and external strife and experience the peace that Jesus offers.

During the few weeks that I was going through an edit of this Bible study, I took a fall one day after I had helped Tommy secure a gas grill on the back of his truck. In getting off the tailgate, I put my hands down and plopped my feet onto the pavement, forgetting that the day before I had pulled the groin muscle in my right leg. When my feet hit the pavement, my injured leg gave way, and I tumbled backward onto the pavement, my head bouncing as I landed.

I had no symptoms of a problem until six days later when I began having headaches, but they weren't bad headaches. Over the next week they got worse, so I finally went to our local hospital's ER. After doing a CT scan, they discovered I had a subdural hematoma and they took me by ambulance to Savannah where there was a team of neurosurgeons. After a night in their ER and another scan, they decided the bleeding had stopped and I just needed to rest for two weeks and then have another follow-up scan to see if the blood in my brain had been absorbed by the surrounding tissue.

This was a scary time for me as I'd never experienced anything like this. My research of exactly what a subdural hematoma was only yielded feelings of fear. One night during the following week, as I was trying to go to sleep, I became overwhelmed with fear that this might not be all right. I remembered these four titles given to Jesus, and I prayed this prayer: "Lord Jesus, as my Wonderful Counselor, I can tell You my fears and know that You understand them and You assure me that You love me and that You've got this, no matter what happens. As Mighty God, I can know without a doubt that You have the power to heal me and that You will if it's in Your plan. As my Everlasting Father, I can feel Your love and comfort as You wrap Your arms of protection around me and show me how very much You care for me. As my Prince of Peace, You wash away my fears and fill me with Your peace. I trust You to help me through this ordeal and I thank You for all You are to me. In Jesus's precious and holy name I pray, amen."

After I finished that prayer, I rolled over and went to sleep, sleeping like a baby all night because of the peace that Jesus gave me. I've shared this with you in case you are facing an overwhelming trial to encourage you to call on Jesus in all these facets of His nature.

We've seen from these four names of Jesus that He really is all we need. **He's our Wonderful Counselor to guide us, He's our Mighty God to accomplish for or through us whatever is His will, He's our Everlasting Father to love and protect us, and He's our Prince of Peace to give us a quality of life that we can only have through Him.** This should give us cause to celebrate every day for the rest of our lives and lead us into eternity already celebrating.

Meditate today on these words from Isaiah 9:6: "And his name shall be called Wonderful Counselor, Mighty God, Everlasting Father, Prince of Peace." Look for opportunities throughout the day to see how these titles apply to your circumstances and spend some time thanking God for giving you such a complete relationship that truly encompasses all you need.

Notes

Day Fourteen—The Message

⁸And in the same region there were shepherds out in the field, keeping watch over their flock by night. ⁹And an angel of the Lord appeared to them, and the glory of the Lord shone around them, and they were filled with great fear. ¹⁰And the angel said to them, "Fear not, for behold, I bring you good news of great joy that will be for all the people. ¹¹For unto you is born this day in the city of David a Savior, who is Christ the Lord. ¹²And this will be a sign for you: you will find a baby wrapped in swaddling cloths and lying in a manger."

—Luke 2:8–12

Today we will focus on the part of the angel's message that says, "I bring you good news of great joy that will be for all the people." We will break this message down into three parts.

First, "I bring you good news" is the way the angel reassured the shepherds that they had nothing to fear and introduced what he was about to tell them. This was not only good news—it was the greatest news ever told because finally man would be able to be redeemed from sin and reconciled to God through a personal relationship.

Read the following passages and record what each one says about good news:

"The light of the eyes rejoices the heart, and good news refreshes the bones" (Proverbs 15:30).

"Like cold water to a thirsty soul, so is good news from a far country" (Proverbs 25:25).

From these passages, we can see that the good news of Jesus Christ has a twofold purpose—it restores health to our bones and gives nourishment to our souls. Therefore, it gives us the physical strength and the spiritual wisdom to carry out God's purpose for which He created us.

Isaiah 61 has much to say about the effect of the good news on man. Verses 1–3 say this:

> [1]The Spirit of the Lord God is upon me, because the Lord has anointed me to bring good news to the poor; he has sent me to bind up the brokenhearted, to proclaim liberty to the captives, and the opening of the prison to those who are bound; [2]to proclaim the year of the Lord's favor, and the day of vengeance of our God; to comfort all who mourn; [3]to grant to those who mourn in Zion—to give them a beautiful headdress instead of ashes, the oil of gladness instead of mourning, the garment of praise instead of a faint spirit; that they may be called oaks of righteousness, the planting of the Lord, that he may be glorified.

We see that the good news provides the following for those who grieve:

Verse 3 says the following will be granted to those who mourn: A beautiful _____ instead of ashes, the oil of

_____ instead of mourning, and a garment of _____ instead of a faint spirit, that they will be called oaks of _____, the planting of the Lord that He may be _____.

The result of the good news, then, is that others are able to see the glory of God.

Acts 5:42 says, "And every day, in the temple and from house to house, they did not cease teaching and preaching that the Christ is Jesus." What is the good news?

_____

What did the apostles do with the good news?

_____

The second part of the angel's message, "of great joy," is the way the angel described the message he was about to bring. It was a message that would make available to mankind a true joy that cannot be experienced aside from a personal relationship with Jesus Christ. This joy is available to all who receive the gift of Jesus.

Psalm 16:11 says, "You make known to me the path of life; in your presence there is fullness of joy; at your right hand are pleasures forevermore." Where is joy found?

_____

Psalm 119:111 says, "Your testimonies are my heritage forever, for they are the joy of my heart." What is the joy of the psalmist?

_____

Psalm 92:4 says, "For you, O Lord, have made me glad by your work; at the works of your hands I sing for joy." What is a reason for joy? _____

_____

John 15:9–11 says, "⁹As the Father has loved me, so have I loved you. Abide in my love. ¹⁰If you keep my commandments, you will abide in my love, just as I have kept my Father's commandments and abide in his love. ¹¹These things I have spoken to you, that my joy may be in you, and that your joy may be full." What comes before joy?

Obedience to God's commands yields true joy. If this joy is present in your heart, and it should be if you are a child of God and are living according to His ways, this joy will be manifested in your countenance. I am amazed at the number of Christians who seem so "unjoyful." Examine your heart and evaluate your joy. What is not inside cannot come out, but what is inside will come out.

Isaiah 55:12 says, "For you shall go out in joy and be led forth in peace." Therefore, because of the joy that comes from the Holy Spirit's indwelling us, we are able to share the good news of Jesus Christ with joy. That leads us to the next point.

Third, "that will be for all the people" tells us that the angel knew this good news was not for just these people at this time, but for all people of all times. John 3:16 says, "For God so loved the _____ that he gave his only Son, that _____ believes in him should not perish but have eternal life." Jesus was not sent for the select few, but for everyone.

Have you surrounded yourself so well with Christian friends that you have isolated yourself from those who need to hear the good news? Luke 4:43 tells of Jesus's response when the people around him tried to keep Him with them. He said, "I must preach the good news of the kingdom of God to the other towns as well, for I was sent for this purpose." Too often we get sidetracked from our purposes by what we are doing where we are. What can you do to expand your territory so that you can reach others with the good news?

Another perspective of this part of the message is that of our selecting to whom we will witness. Have you ever not witnessed to someone because you thought he or she would not be interested in hearing the good news? It is not for us to decide who will respond and who will not; we cannot possibly know that. It is simply our responsibility to tell them. Mark 16:15–16 says, "¹⁵And he said to them, 'Go into all the world and proclaim the Gospel to the whole creation. ¹⁶Whoever believes and is baptized will be saved, but whoever does not believe will be condemned.'" And Romans 10:14 says, "How then will they call on him in whom they have not believed? And how are they to believe in him of whom they have never heard? And how are they to hear without someone preaching?"

Because of the good news of the birth of Jesus Christ, we should be filled with joy and want to tell everyone so they, too, can know Him. Allow that fact to so permeate your heart and mind that it pushes out any thoughts or values that are not in line with Jesus's teachings and the purpose for which He came.

Meditate today on this part of Luke 2:10: "I bring you good news of great joy that will be for all the people." Focus today on that fact: that this truly is good news of great joy that is available for all people! Make sure that you are obedient to God's commands today so that you have true joy, and be alert to opportunities to share Christ with others. Also, thank God for sending His Son to be born in the flesh so that you have good news which you can share with others out of a heart full of joy.

Notes

Day Fifteen—Glory for God and Peace for Man

¹³And suddenly there was with the angel a multitude of the heavenly host praising God and saying, ¹⁴"Glory to God in the highest, and on earth peace among those with whom he is pleased!"

—Luke 2:13–14

What we should see in this passage about the birth of Jesus is twofold:

1. God is glorified.
2. Peace is available to those with whom God is pleased.

John 1:14 says, "And the Word became flesh and dwelt among us, and we have seen his glory, glory as of the only Son from the Father, full of grace and truth." The "Word" is Jesus and John indicates that to have seen Jesus was to see His glory. Then skipping to the last three words of this verse, His glory was full of what two attributes? _____ and _____.

John 2 records the miracle in which Jesus turned water into wine and verse 11 follows the story with these words: "This, the first of his signs, Jesus did at Cana in Galilee, and manifested his glory. And his disciples believed in him." How did Jesus reveal the glory of God?

John 15:5–8 says,

> [5]I am the vine; you are the branches. Whoever abides in me and I in him, he it is that bears much fruit, for apart from me you can do nothing. [6]If anyone does not abide in me he is thrown away like a branch and withers; and the branches are gathered, thrown into the fire, and burned. [7]If you abide in me, and my words abide in you, ask whatever you wish, and it will be done for you. [8]By this my Father is glorified, that you bear much fruit and so prove to be my disciples.

How does Jesus say that God is glorified?_____

_____

God knew His plan before the creation of the world. He knew that He would send His only Son to die as payment for the sins of mankind. It's incredible to think about how God loved sinful man to such an extent that He was actually willing to allow His only Son to leave the glory of heaven and become a man where He would be mocked, laughed at, spat upon, and finally crucified by the very people He had come to save. Yet, in all of this, God was glorified through the life of Jesus because He was the embodiment of grace and truth. How does this apply to us?

As children of God, we are responsible for emulating His character—for manifesting His grace and truth in everything we do. God's glory is revealed in us as we allow the Holy Spirit to work miracles in our hearts, empowering us to live according to God's principles and not the world's. His glory is revealed in us when we love others the way He loves them and when we extend mercy and grace instead of criticism and judgment. Finally, His glory is revealed in us when others see God in us.

Part of manifesting God's glory, His grace and truth, concerns our appearance—the outward way we portray God. Our appearance is an indicator of what is happening on the inside; it is also the first thing people see even before our actions. A smile can radiate God's love and grace in a powerful way. It indicates our inward joy, along with our love and value for another person. If you want to make other people feel valued, look at them, smile at them, and speak to them.

Another way we manifest God's glory is in our dress. We should always remember that as God's children, we represent Him everywhere we go. For this reason, we should always take care to look in a way that represents Him well. Our clothes don't have to be the finest made, but they should be neat and appropriate. I grew up with parents who instilled in my brother and me that we should always do our very best, and that included our appearances. It starts on the inside, but it overflows to the outside. Is God glorified in your appearance?

The second part of the angel's message was "and on earth peace among those with whom he is pleased!" Who are those with whom God is pleased?

There's a tendency to think of this peace as being peace between all people; however, there will never be that kind of peace on earth on this side of heaven. Matthew 10:34 records these words of Jesus: "Do not think that I have come to bring peace to the earth. I have not come to bring peace, but a sword." Jesus went on to describe the division that would come to families because of Him. However, the peace that the angel spoke of was peace between a person and God, the peace that we can only have through a relationship with God through His Son Jesus. **The essence of Christmas is that Jesus came to reconcile people to God. We were created in such a way that true peace is only possible through this relationship, so this peace the angel spoke of is a very big deal.**

Another description used in the Bible for one with whom God is pleased is one who found favor with God. One example of such a man is found in Genesis 6:8-9, which says, "But Noah found favor

Sherry Myers

in the eyes of the Lord. ⁹These are the generations of Noah. Noah
was a righteous man, blameless in his generation. Noah walked
with God." Noah was obviously one who pleased God and we
can assume he experienced peace with God as he obeyed God's
command concerning the ark, not peace with man but peace with
God. How does this passage describe Noah?

_____

Read John 15:9–17 below and circle every occurrence of *love*
or *loved*.

⁹As the Father has loved me, so have I loved you.
Abide in my love. ¹⁰If you keep my commandments,
you will abide in my love, just as I have kept my
Father's commandments and abide in his love.
¹¹These things I have spoken to you, that my joy
may be in you, and that your joy may be full. ¹²This
is my commandment, that you love one another as
I have loved you. ¹³Greater love has no one than
this, that someone lay down his life for his friends.
¹⁴You are my friends if you do what I command
you. ¹⁵No longer do I call you servants, for the
servant does not know what his master is doing;
but I have called you friends, for all that I have
heard from my Father I have made known to you.
¹⁶You did not choose me, but I chose you and
appointed you that you should go and bear fruit
and that your fruit should abide, so that whatever
you ask the Father in my name, he may give it to
you. ¹⁷These things I command you, so that you
will love one another.

How many times did the words *love* or *loved* occur? _____
What does that tell you?

This passage holds the key to pleasing God. I believe it can be summarized in these words: "Love God and love each other; obey God and experience His joy." First, the source of this love is Jesus, as illustrated by the vine. Second, our love for Jesus results in our obedience to His commands (fruit bearing). Third, our obedience results in joy. Therefore, you can see the following pattern:

Love $\Rightarrow$ Obedience $\Rightarrow$ Joy

Through this pattern, God is glorified, and we are joyful. What could be better than that?

Back to our focus passage for today, Luke 2:13-14, what is available to those with whom God is pleased? _____

_____

Numerous times in scripture, the words *peace* and *joy* are used together. They go hand-in-hand because it would be difficult, if not impossible, to have one without the other. The Greek word used for *peace* is *eirene,* which means "peace, tranquility, repose, calm, harmony, accord, well-being, prosperity." The Hebrew-Greek Key Word Study Bible goes further to describe it this way: "Such a state of peace is the object of divine promise and is brought about by God's mercy, granting deliverance and freedom from all the distresses that are experienced as a result of sin. **Hence, the message of salvation is called the gospel of peace, for this peace can only be the result of reconciliation with God.**" (Emphasis added) God knew when He created us that we would sin, but it was not His will for us to be trapped in it. He provided a way out through His Son Jesus so that we can experience freedom instead of captivity.

Psalm 55:22 says, "Cast your burden on the Lord, and he will sustain you; he will never permit the righteous to be moved." What are we told to do with our cares?

As a result, what will God do for us?

We have the promise that if we cast our cares on Him, He will sustain us. He will never let the righteous fall. The key word is *righteous*. The only way we can be righteous is by the blood of Jesus. You must be His child in order to have His peace. As His child, His peace is available to you, no matter what you are going through. It is not His intention that you should be consumed with worry. This casting is a conscious act on our part. It is a decision we make to give our worries to Him. He will not force them out of our clenched hands, but He will accept them when we give them to Him with open hands. Why not give your problems to the One who is in control and can work them out far better than you could even if you had the power?

Meditate today on Luke 2:14: "Glory to God in the highest, and on earth peace among those with whom he is pleased." Ask God to help you glorify Him in all that you do and remember that His peace is available to you as you give Him your troubles. Thank God for this glorious gift.

Notes

Day Sixteen—An Excited Response

> ¹⁶And they went with haste and found Mary and Joseph, and the baby lying in a manger. ¹⁷And when they saw it, they made known the saying that had been told them concerning this child. ¹⁸And all who heard it wondered at what the shepherds told them. ¹⁹But Mary treasured up all these things, pondering them in her heart. ²⁰And the shepherds returned, glorifying and praising God for all they had heard and seen, as it had been told them.
>
> —Luke 2:16–20

Today's passage is broken down into two parts: the shepherds' response to the message about Jesus and their response to being in the presence of Jesus.

The Response to the Message

First, this passage says that, in response to the message of the angels, the shepherds "_____ _____ _____ and found Mary and Joseph and the baby." They were anxious to see this Savior whose birth had caused the angels of heaven to glorify God. Why do you think they hurried?

_____

_____

I believe it was because they were excited about the possibility of being in the presence of the Savior of the world. Do we share the good news of Jesus with such excitement that non-Christians rush to Him, they can't wait to know more about this person who has changed our life? Next, on a scale of 1–10, how would you rate your excitement about spending time in the presence of this Savior? _____ He's no longer a baby in a manger—He's fulfilled His role as Savior of the world. We have a clearer picture of exactly who He is than the shepherds had that night, so we have even more reason to be excited. Yet I'm afraid that so many of us look at our relationship with Him with such apathy that it pales in comparison to our relationships with others.

When you really think about your ability to spend time with the God of the universe, allowing Him to teach you His truths and pour into you His wisdom, the privilege of it should certainly excite you, to say the least! The gift of Jesus is what made that possible. The shepherds immediately left their flocks and went searching for Jesus. They didn't take time to "clean up their lives first" or get sidetracked with insignificant tasks. They simply hurried off to find Jesus. God wants us to seek Him just as we are and allow Him to change us where we need to be changed. Ask God to excite you about spending time with Him and begin to approach your time with God with renewed excitement and anticipation of what He will say to you and how He will transform you into the person He wants you to be.

The second point of the response of the shepherds to the message is that they found Mary, Joseph, and the baby Jesus. Anyone who seeks Jesus will find Him. It is not God's intention to hide His precious gift, making the decision to accept Him difficult. His Gift of Jesus is so simple, so readily available to all that many will miss it because of the simplicity of it. Even we Christians may feel at times that God is not there, but you can rest assured that He is. He doesn't leave us or forsake us.

Proverbs 8:17 says, "I love those who love me, and those who seek me diligently find me." What is God's feeling for those who

seek Him? _____ How are we to seek Him?
_____What happens for those who seek
Him? _____

Can we ask any more than to be loved by God and find Him
when we seek Him? That says it all. So the appropriate response to
the message of Jesus is to immediately seek Him.

The Response to Being in the Presence of Jesus

We also see in today's passage the two-part response of the
shepherds to seeing the baby Jesus. Their lives were deeply touched
from being in the presence of the Savior of the world. What was
their response? First, they spread the word concerning what had
been told them about this child. If we have truly had an experience
of salvation and are able to experience the presence of God, we
will not be able to keep from telling others about Him. Sharing
good news is a natural response. How in the world, then, can one
spend time in the presence of Jesus, the Savior of the world, and be
untouched and unchanged? The only way we can do that is to fail to
recognize who He is. Possibly many of us go through the motions
of prayer and Bible study without earnestly seeking Jesus. Ask God
to give you an intense knowledge of who He really is and, with that,
a desire to share Him with others.

The second part of the shepherds' response to being in the
presence of Jesus is their act of glorifying and praising God. A
natural outcome of being in the presence of Jesus and sharing Him
with others is glorifying and praising Him. A life that glorifies and
praises God is certainly a life that pleases Him and continues to be
used by Him.

How touched are you by the message about Jesus and being
in His presence? Do you eagerly anticipate the opportunity to
experience His presence—whether it's in your favorite place for
your personal time with Him or in corporate worship where you
sing praises to Him and hear His Word preached? **Do you do the**

same as the shepherds—excitedly seek Him, spread the word, glorify and praise God? Pray that God will give you a seeking heart, then a sharing heart that also glorifies and praises God.

Meditate today on these phrases from Luke 2:16 and 20: "[16]And they went with haste and found Mary and Joseph, and the baby, lying in a manger … [20]And the shepherds returned, glorifying and praising God for all they had heard and seen, as it had been told them." Throughout the day, ask God to give you a sense of urgency and excitement about spending time with Him, about the realization that He is with you all the time, as well as an intense desire to share Him with others, and, finally, a countenance that glorifies and praises Him. Thank Him for sending His Son to be born in the flesh so that you and anyone else who accepts Jesus can know God.

Notes

Day Seventeen—Consecrated

²¹On the eighth day, when it was time to circumcise the child, he was named Jesus, the name the angel had given him before he was conceived. ²²When the time came for the purification rites required by the Law of Moses, Joseph and Mary took him to Jerusalem to present him to the Lord ²³(as it is written in the Law of the Lord, 'Every firstborn male is to be consecrated to the Lord'), ²⁴and to offer a sacrifice in keeping with what is said in the Law of the Lord: "a pair of doves or two young pigeons." Luke 2:21–24 (NIV)

(Sherry's note: Of all the topics we've covered so far in this study, this day's topic of being consecrated has been the most life-changing concept for me personally. I pray that you will not just read through this, but will prayerfully consider how God wants you to consecrate yourself to Him and His service. I acknowledge that this day's material is longer than the other days, but please don't miss the truths that are in these passages.)

Today we will look at what it means to be consecrated and will consider two aspects of Jesus's being consecrated—the first concerning his example of a person consecrated to God and the second concerning the example of Mary and Joseph as parents consecrating this child to God. There were two Greek words used for the word *consecrated*. One is *kaleo*, which means "to set apart for a specific task." The other is *hagios,* which means "holy, sacred, separated from ordinary or common usage and devoted to God."

Looking at the background of this practice, we see in Exodus 13:2 this message God gave Moses: "Consecrate to me all the firstborn. Whatever is the first to open the womb among the people of Israel, both of man and of beast, is mine." This was right after God had miraculously delivered the Israelites from the Egyptian bondage. He had slain the firstborn of the Egyptians and protected the firstborn children of the Israelites, so He instituted this ritual to serve as a reminder of His deliverance of His people. Just as the blood from lambs was put on the doorposts of the Israelites' homes to spare their firstborn, Jesus would later become the sacrifice whose blood would spare all who would receive it from eternal destruction and grant them eternal life in heaven. Mary and Joseph would have had no idea all that this consecration of Jesus would mean, but they knew that He belonged to God, and this was their way of acknowledging that.

This act of consecrating was not just for the firstborn, as we see in many passages throughout scripture. Leviticus 20:7 says, "Consecrate yourselves, therefore, and be holy, for I am the LORD your God." What specific command are we given in this verse?

What is the reason for this command?

The Hebrew word used for *consecrate* in this verse is *qadas,* which means "to be holy, sacred, dedicated and consecrated." It denotes a decision to be set aside and used exclusively for God. Most of us are probably more familiar with the term *dedicated* than we are *consecrated.* So then, consider what you think about a person who is dedicated to a sports team. How would you describe his or her dedication?

What activities and attitudes would make you use the phrase that they are dedicated to their team?

_____

_____

Also, married couples are hopefully dedicated to each other because of their love for and commitment to each other. Good employees are dedicated to the company for which they work. Some people are said to be dedicated to their church or civic organization to which they belong. However, dedication to sports teams, jobs, or organizations or even another person is not the same level of dedication or consecration meant by this word. The reason is that this term includes being *holy and sacred* in our dedication or consecration. To be consecrated to God brings about a whole new level of dedication. This is a level that we absolutely cannot attain on our own; it is only attained by the Holy Spirit working in and through us to make us holy.

Developing consecrated believers was the goal of Jesus's teaching ministry. Just before He was betrayed by Judas, Jesus spent time praying a prayer recorded in John 17. He spent a great deal of this prayer praying for those who had become His followers, and he referred to them as "mine." Read His words recorded in John 17:15–19: "[15] I do not ask that you take them out of the world, but that you keep them from the evil one. [16] They are not of the world, just as I am not of the world. [17] Sanctify them in the truth; your word is truth. [18] As you sent me into the world, so I have sent them into the world. [19] And for their sake I consecrate myself, that they also may be sanctified in truth." Jesus longed for His followers to consecrate themselves, to be used exclusively for Him, so they could carry out what He had begun.

As I prayed about this word *consecrated*, asking God to give me wisdom to know what it really means to be consecrated, the passage that came to mind was Mary's words recorded in Luke 1:46–48: "My soul magnifies the Lord, [47]and my spirit rejoices in God my Savior,

[48] for he has looked on the humble estate of his servant." Think about the word *magnifies* for a moment. To magnify something means it is enlarged and made clearer just as a magnifying glass enlarges things so they can be seen more easily.

Lived out in the life of a believer, magnifying God becomes the revealing of God to the world—a way for the world to see God's love, joy, peace, grace, and mercy. This is characteristic of a person consecrated to God, a person who has surrendered himself to God as on an altar for the purpose of magnifying and glorifying Him. It is not simply a mind shift; it is a deep longing that reaches to the core of who we are, our soul longing intensely to magnify, glorify God and it stems from our recognition of who we are and who He is. In true humility, we choose to lift Him up, to make sure He is glorified in all we do. How do we attain this level of consecration?

First, of course, we must begin by accepting Jesus's sacrifice as payment for our sins and repenting of our sins, committing our lives to follow Him.

Second, we allow God's Holy Spirit who lives in us to make us holy. When we accept Jesus Christ as our Savior, the Holy Spirit comes to live in us. However, He doesn't steamroll us into being holy; He transforms us into holiness when we submit to Him and allow Him control over us. As we grow spiritually, we turn over more and more of ourselves to God's control through His Holy Spirit. We must willingly agree to be set aside and used exclusively for God if we really want to live a life with meaning that will last for eternity. This means that we obey God's commands and seek to make sure that what we do is in line with God's purpose for our lives. It doesn't mean that we're perfect, because we know we can't be, but we are sensitive to our disobedience when it happens, and we confess our sins and accept God's forgiveness for them.

Being consecrated to God involves sacrificing ourselves—our wants, our plans—for what God wants. Romans 12:1–2 says, "[1] I appeal to you therefore, brothers, by the mercies of God, to present your bodies as a living sacrifice, holy and acceptable to God, which is your spiritual worship. [2]Do not be conformed to this world, but be transformed by the renewal of your mind, that by testing you may discern what is the will of God, what is good and acceptable and perfect."

The Israelites placed a high value on sacrifices because of their enabling them to be clean before God. We don't make the same kind of sacrifice because our sins have been atoned for by the blood of Jesus. However, that doesn't mean that we are not to sacrifice. According to this passage, how are we to sacrifice today?

Consider these words in this passage: "a living sacrifice, holy and acceptable to God." Becoming a living sacrifice for God makes us holy and that holiness makes us acceptable to God. Holiness is not a sought-after trait of the secular world; it is life on a whole different plane than what is natural in the flesh. Here are some examples of how we display holiness if we live at this level:

1. We seek to look at life from God's perspective as best we can from studying His Word and applying it to our lives.
2. We treat all others with love and respect, as the people loved by God that they are.
3. We react to mistreatment with grace and forgiveness and a willingness to overlook the wrong.
4. When confrontation is needed, we handle it with a godly spirit, seeking His resolution.
5. We do all we can to represent God well by the smile on our face and our outward appearance.
6. We take a stand for what is right in a godly way, speaking truth without attacking the character of the other person.
7. We place a higher priority on relationships than on any material possessions.

8. We set our own feelings and desires aside to press on toward the calling God has placed before us.
9. We trust God to work out His will instead of our manipulating any situation.
10. When we face difficulty with any of the above, we pray, "Help me, Jesus" and allow Him to change our heart and mind.

Maybe you already are living a life that is holy, but in case you wouldn't describe your life that way, write examples of what in your life you would describe as holy and what you would describe as unholy. Then ask God to give you the ability to relinquish control and allow the Holy Spirit greater rein over your life.

There's an old hymn written by Johnson Oatman Jr. and published in 1898 called "Higher Ground." Here are the words:

I'm pressing on the upward way, new heights I'm gaining every day;
Still praying as I'm onward bound, Lord, plant my feet on higher ground.

My heart has no desire to stay where doubts arise and fears dismay;
Though some may dwell where these abound, my prayer, my aim is higher ground.

I want to live above the world, though Satan's darts at me are hurled;
For faith has caught the joyful sound, the song of saints on higher ground.

I want to scale the utmost height and catch a gleam
of glory bright;
But still I'll pray, 'til heaven I've found, "Lord, lead
me on to higher ground."

Chorus:
Lord, lift me up and let me stand by faith on
heaven's tableland,
A higher plane than I have found; Lord, plant my
feet on higher ground.

This great old hymn expresses so well the heart of a person consecrated to God, living a life wrapped in His holiness and focused on praising and glorifying Him. This is a life that refuses to be bogged down by the stresses of Satan's darts and focuses on what really is important—living on a higher plane of surrender to God. This concept reminds me of the saying, "living above the fray." I used to wonder what that meant, but spiritually, it means living above the junk that the world wants to use to bog us down. If our soul's desire is glorifying God, we don't have to stress about everything that comes along, and when we get confused, we seek God's wisdom. We also don't have to try to figure out if certain things are permissible—our question becomes, "Is it holy?" Some things are permissible but not holy.

The second aspect of the consecration of Jesus is that of Mary and Joseph as his earthly parents dedicating Him to God. They traveled the six-mile distance from Bethlehem to Jerusalem to consecrate their son to God and to offer the appropriate sacrifice. The consecration was their way of dedicating to God the child He had given them. They knew that Jesus was different from any other child; they had been told by the angel that He would be the Messiah. However, they really could not have understood all that His life would involve. They did all that they knew to do at the time. That is all that God expects of us today.

As parents, we should follow the example of Mary and Joseph and dedicate the children that God blesses us with to Him and ask Him to bring about His perfect plan for their lives. That dedication should involve our giving them to Him so completely that we allow Him to work in their lives even when we don't understand or agree. It involves the realization that our children belong to God, and while we have a responsibility to be the godly parents that He wants us to be, our control is limited. He has a plan for them just as He has a plan for us, and we should never interfere with His plan for the lives of our children.

If you're a parent, have you given your child or children to God and realized the limitation of your role as a parent? _____ Are you willing to accept God's plan for your children's lives even if it is different from your plan for their lives? _____ Do you pray daily for God to work out His perfect plan in their lives? _____

In 2013, our son, Brett, was a pastor in Westminster, South Carolina, which was just a little over an hour from where we lived in Gainesville, Georgia. Christie, our daughter, was single and lived in Cumming, Georgia, just forty-five minutes from us. Brett and his wife, Kristin, had begun to feel God calling them to plant a church somewhere and were diligently seeking God's will for where that would be. That summer, God revealed to them that He wanted them to move to Calgary, Alberta, and plant a church in a new community there. They had two daughters, ages two and four, and Kristin was pregnant with their third daughter. We were on a mission trip to Calgary with Brett and some of his church members when God revealed that call to him.

The same week, even before we had any idea that God was calling them there, God spoke to Tommy and me and told us He wanted us to spend the summers there helping with mission teams and summer camps when Tommy retired in March of 2014. Later in the week when Brett shared his call with us, we were astounded and honored that God would work in all our hearts that way—giving us a love for the people there and a desire to tell them about Jesus and enjoying the privilege of working alongside Brett and Kristin in the summers as they ministered to the people there. The week after we returned home from that mission trip, Christie told us that God was calling her to spend a year in Roatan, Honduras, working with children with special needs. Roatan is an island off the coast of Honduras and, although it has beautiful beaches and mountains, it also has extreme poverty and children with special needs had no source of help or training. It is also not the safest place in the world to live.

So within two weeks, we found out that both our children and our precious daughter-in-law and granddaughters were moving out of the country in totally opposite directions! This could have been devastating, but the peace and satisfaction that God gave us was just incredible. We knew that they really weren't "our kids" as much as they were "God's kids." What a joy we have when our children are obedient to God's call even when it comes with sacrifice on our parts. We were able to spend the next four summers in Calgary helping Brett and Kristin serve the mission teams and conduct summer camps for the children. We were also able to spend time in Roatan with Christie serving the people there. Yes, it was sad to have them so far away, but knowing they were in the center of God's will far surpassed the fact that we weren't physically together more often. We knew that we had all eternity to be together and it was important to do in this life what God called each of us to do.

Four years later, in 2018, God blessed us way above our wildest imagination when He brought Brett and Kristin and their four daughters, for him to be our pastor at First Baptist Church of Hilton Head Island, and then led Christie and her husband, Brandon, to also move to the island. We've learned to never cease to be amazed at the working of God!

I've shared our story with you to encourage you who have children whom God calls to serve Him in distant places or in vocations that aren't your choosing. Rejoice in the fact that your children want to be obedient to God and support their decision. Above all, acknowledge that they are His children and trust Him to use them and care for them.

We have seen from today's study that Jesus, even from His birth, gave us the example that we are to follow if we are to be pleasing to God. God had a very special purpose for His life, but He also has a special and different purpose for our lives. We are to consecrate ourselves for that purpose. Then, as parents, we should consecrate our children to God and relinquish them to His control.

Meditate today on Leviticus 20:7: "Consecrate yourselves, therefore, and be holy, for I am the Lord your God." Throughout the day, ask God to make you constantly aware that this is a two-part process that involves your part—being given to God's service—and His part—making you holy. Thank Him for His promises throughout His Word that when we do our part, He will do His.

Notes

Day Eighteen—Disturbed

¹After Jesus was born in Bethlehem in Judea, during the time of King Herod, Magi from the east came to Jerusalem ²and asked, "Where is the one who has been born king of the Jews? We saw his star when it rose and have come to worship him." ³When King Herod heard this he was disturbed, and all Jerusalem with him.

—Matthew 2:1-3 (NIV)

Reread the last sentence of the above passage. Why was King Herod disturbed?

_____

_____

This birth of Jesus obviously threatened King Herod's spirit because he was the king of Judea. Of course, he would not want someone else to take over as king, especially someone outside his family and not in line to follow him. It's easy for us to see this in him. However, all of us in our sinful natures have ourselves on the throne of our hearts and also feel threatened at the prospect of someone else taking over that throne. The threat to King Herod prompted him to have many young boys murdered all across his land. This same threat can also cause us to do or say things that are not in line with God's character. Therefore, today we will look at the threat that Jesus's being king makes to all of us in our sinful nature's desire to be our own king.

This threat to kingship is the common thread that runs through all people who have not accepted Jesus's reign over their lives and even some of us who have. Until we understand that God loves us and has a wonderful plan for us that He wants to help us fulfill, it's difficult for us to yield our lives to Him. Tommy and I have a dear friend who truly desires to be in such control of his own destiny that he's unwilling to yield any control to anyone, even God. He owns his own company for this reason. He wants to choose the plan for his life and live each day as he desires. It's easier for us who know God through a personal relationship with Jesus to understand the concept of God's love and His plan for our lives, but this is a very difficult concept for some non-Christians to understand. It's one, though, that if not grasped, will come at a price far greater than anyone will want to pay.

This passage concerning Herod helps me to understand the reluctance of non-Christians to accept Jesus as their Lord and Savior. They want to be their own king, their own authority in control of their own destiny. The sad part is that their control over their own destiny gets them death and eternal separation from God. Only God can take away that disturbing feeling and convict them of their need for Him. When King Herod died, he faced God with an even more disturbing feeling! He faced judgment from the one who had been sent to give him deliverance. King Herod truly was in control of his own destiny, and it did not have a pretty ending.

Non-Christians living today will face that same destiny unless they realize who Jesus really is and accept Him as Savior and King. Will we help them understand? Will we help them see Jesus as the King who loves them and wants to deliver them from themselves and from eternal separation from God? If only we could help people know peace rather than disturbance, we would be successful in something of eternal value. Think of someone you know who is not a Christian and ask God to give you a way to help them with this issue of disturbance over God's desire to reign in his or her life.

We can't leave this topic without pointing out that if non-Christians saw more Christians living with the love, joy, grace, peace and mercy that only come from God, maybe they wouldn't be so reluctant to give themselves to Him. Think about that for a few moments. Do people see God in you? As we discussed yesterday, do you reveal Him to everyone around you in a way that should make them want to know the God you serve?

That brings us to the second aspect of this "disturbance" that concerns Christians. We have accepted Jesus's salvation, but have we truly accepted Jesus's reign, His authority over our lives? Describe a time when you had difficulty allowing God to be the King over all your life.

When we feel the power of the Holy Spirit leading us in a direction that opposes our sinful nature or just simply our own desires, it is natural to feel uncomfortable. That is when obedience should win out and transform our discomfort into victory. Have you ever fretted and fretted over a situation because it wasn't going your way? These times can be avoided if we simply trust God to do what He wants to do and lead us in the way He wants us to go. When we try to manipulate situations in our favor, we're taking over His place of King and the natural result will be disturbed feelings leading to unhappiness and lost blessings. We have then allowed the evil one to steal us of the joy we are meant to have.

Jesus is King, and He has all authority because it has been given Him by God—"And Jesus came and said to them, 'All authority in heaven and on earth has been given to me.'" Matthew 28:18. **We must accept the kingship of Jesus over our lives in order to be obedient to Him and fulfill the purposes He has for us. When that is accomplished, the disturbed feeling is replaced with true peace and joy.**

Meditate today on Matthew 2:3: "When King Herod heard this he was disturbed, and all Jerusalem with him." (NIV) Throughout the day, ask God for two things. Ask Him to help you enjoy His peace instead of disturbance by allowing Him to reign in your life. Then ask Him to make you sensitive to those around you who may be disturbed at the thought of relinquishing control to God's reign over their lives. Allow Him to use you as His vessel to be poured out so that His peace and joy are visible to those around you. Thank God for sending His Son who delivers you from uneasy, disturbing feelings into His glorious peace.

Notes

Day Nineteen—The Wrong Advisor

¹Now after Jesus was born in Bethlehem of Judea in the days of Herod the king, behold, wise men from the east came to Jerusalem, ²saying, "Where is he who has been born king of the Jews? For we saw his star when it rose and have come to worship him' ...
¹³Now when they had departed, behold, an angel of the Lord appeared to Joseph in a dream and said, "Rise, take the child and his mother, and flee to Egypt, and remain there until I tell you, for Herod is about to search for the child, to destroy him."

—Matthew 2:1–2, 13

The focus of our study today is the seriousness of seeking the wrong counsel. God had given the Magi a star to direct them to Jesus. However, when they arrived in Jerusalem, they may have assumed that the king would know where this new king of the Jews had been born. It probably seemed easier to just ask him than to follow the star.

Matthew 2:9 says, "After listening to the king, they went on their way. And behold, the star that they had seen when it rose went before them until it came to rest over the place where the child was." How did they find Jesus?

The star had been there all the time; all they had to do was follow it. Isn't the same true of us today? We don't follow a star literally, but God directs us by His Word and His Holy Spirit. Can you recall a time when you knew what you needed to do, but you allowed yourself to ask someone else and you got sidetracked from the original plan? Describe it.

_____

_____

Psalm 73:24 says, "You guide me with your counsel, and afterward you will receive me to glory."

Psalm 119:9–11 says, "⁹How can a young man keep his way pure? By guarding it according to your word. ¹⁰With my whole heart I seek you; let me not wander from your commandments! ¹¹I have stored up your word in my heart, that I might not sin against you."

John 14:26 says, "But the Helper, the Holy Spirit, whom the Father will send in my name, he will teach you all things and bring to your remembrance all that I have said to you."

Matthew 7:7 says, "Ask, and it will be given to you; seek, and you will find; knock, and it will be opened to you."

When God gives us specific direction from His Word and the Holy Spirit, He expects us to follow His command and not go around asking others what they think about it. He may not have spoken to anyone else about that command in that situation. So if we ask others, even Christians, they may mislead us because they haven't heard from God regarding the particular command. It's like giving our children a command and then having them go around asking other children if they should do it. That seems ridiculous, doesn't it? Yet that's what we do many times to God.

Sometimes when we face a problem or difficult situation, maybe it's a relationship problem, I believe our desire to talk to other people is driven by our desire (maybe unconsciously) to wallow in it, not really solving it. If we could only discipline ourselves to seek God's counsel first, we could spare ourselves and others the wasted time and energy used in unnecessary chatter that leads to nothing profitable. Not only does God want to hear our concerns and problems, but also He has the power to solve them.

I shared on another day about my life passage that I also call my "reset button," which is Hebrews 12:1–2. God has used that passage, along with many others, to speak to me and bring truth to my mind and then apply it to my situation. Every time I've gone to my prayer place and poured my heart out to God, not only has He comforted and encouraged me, but also He's given me direction for what I needed to do. Where I have kneeled down, I have then gotten up refreshed and empowered to face whatever the difficulty.

Let me quickly add one comment here. There are many scriptures that address the value of wise counsel, so I am not saying that we should not seek counsel of other Christians when we are unsure what to do. What I am saying is that when we have the direction and we know what God wants us to do, we should simply do it. Many times it is our flesh that seeks counsel from others out of our dislike for the command; therefore, we think that maybe if we ask others, they will steer us away from the command, and we can justify our disobedience.

Another important point we want to make here is that the Magi sought counsel from a king who was ungodly. When we do seek counsel, it should be only from a Christian who is devoted to God's will and His statutes. The Magi really made two mistakes. First, they had the star to follow, but instead they stopped to ask someone else. Second, that someone else was not devoted to God and His statutes. Can you recall a time when you either sought advice when you really knew what you needed to do or you sought needed advice from the wrong person? If so, describe it.

_____

_____

First Kings 22:5 says, "And Jehoshaphat said to the king of Israel, 'Inquire first for the word of the Lord.'" If we are unsure of the direction we should take, it is God's counsel that we should seek first. It is easy to run to friends for advice before spending time on our faces before God, but that is out of order. In times of uncertainty, spend time with God seeking His counsel and then if you're still unsure about it, ask Him to speak through others around you to confirm His will to you. Looking back at our focal passage for today, what was the consequence of the Magi's seeking counsel from the king?

_____

_____

We don't know what would have happened if they had not done this. Possibly, the king would have heard about it from someone else and would still have had boys under the age of two killed. However, it would not have been on the shoulders of the Magi as a result of their visit to him. Many baby boys were slaughtered because they sought the wrong advisor. There are also consequences for us when we seek the wrong counsel.

God's will should dominate our lives to such an extent that we refuse to lose precious time needed to carry out His will by seeking the counsel of others when we know what to do. Determine right now to focus on following the direction that God has laid out before you.

Meditate today on Psalm 119:35: "Lead me in the path of your commandments, for I delight in it." Throughout the day, ask God to help you obey His commands and avoid the temptation to seek wrong counsel. Thank Him for sending His Son so that you can seek counsel directly from Him.

Notes

Day Twenty—Overjoyed

⁹After they had heard the king, they went on their way, and the star they had seen when it rose went ahead of them until it stopped over the place where the child was. ¹⁰When they saw the star, they were overjoyed. ¹¹On coming to the house, they saw the child with his mother Mary, and they bowed down and worshiped him.

—Matthew 2:9–11a (NIV)

The wise men, or Magi, were seeking the baby Jesus, the one they knew would be the king. Verse 2 gives their reason for seeking Him: "Where is he who has been born king of the Jews? For we saw his star when it rose and have come to worship him." They sought Jesus for the purpose of worshiping Him. When they saw the star and knew they were about to be in the presence of Jesus, they were overjoyed. They were eager to worship Him. Worship flows from a heart of joy, which is the focus of our study today.

What does it mean to be "overjoyed"? Describe it in your words.

_____

Can you say that you usually or sometimes feel overjoyed? _____ If not, can you recall the last time you felt overjoyed? _____ If so, describe it.

_____

To be overjoyed is to possess a joy that is so great that it affects the mind and emotions and it pours out onto our countenance. It's a joy that cannot be contained; it overflows to all those around us. The wise men were overjoyed because they knew they were about to be in the presence of the Messiah. They were ready to worship Him. This tells me that my heart should overflow with the joy of the Lord all the time because the presence of the Lord is with me in the person of the Holy Spirit. That joy should precede my worship—it should lead me into worship.

I've been around Christians who exude that joy, and I've been around Christians who don't. What makes the difference? If Jesus is our source of life and our reason for living, He should also be our source of joy. Many times, we experience what we call joy, but it's really just happiness—a state of feeling happy that is due to circumstances that have gone our way. However, true joy is unrelated to circumstances; it can be present regardless of our circumstances. A test to see if what you have is joy is whether this joy leads you to worship Christ. Joy that comes from an intimate relationship with Christ leads us to worship Him.

We are robbed of our joy when we allow it to be choked out by the many distractions of the world and we try to satisfy our fleshly needs—the need to feel loved and appreciated by others, the need to have certain things, the need to have circumstances go our way, and on and on. If our focus really is on pleasing God and serving Him through the power of the Holy Spirit, we won't have these needs because God will meet all our real needs, and the mind of Christ in us will allow us to see what we once thought of as "needs" as they really are—the flesh. Then we can release those around us from having to do or say certain things to maintain our joy. We will realize that the world really doesn't revolve around us. It revolves around God, who is the center of the universe and the one in control of the universe. It is then that we can experience what it means to be overjoyed. Then what follows that joy is our worship of Christ.

First Peter 4:12–13 says, "¹²Beloved, do not be surprised at the fiery trial when it comes upon you to test you, as though something strange were happening to you. ¹³But rejoice insofar as you share Christ's sufferings, that you may also rejoice and be glad when his glory is revealed." Rewrite this passage in your own words.

_____

_____

_____

Because God sent His only Son to be born in the flesh and because He suffered for our sins, Jesus Christ is glorified. A key phrase of the above passage is "that you may also rejoice and be glad when his glory is revealed." Whether we are asked to suffer in small or great ways for the cause of Christ, His glory can be revealed through our sufferings, and the result of that is our rejoicing or being overjoyed. Have you ever suffered for the cause of Christ? Or when you've experienced pain or difficulty, did you rejoice in it because of what God was going to do in you and others as a result of it? Describe a time that comes to mind.

_____

_____

Spend a few minutes examining your "joy level." Do you think that others consistently see in you the joy of the Lord, regardless of your circumstances? Since this emotion of being overjoyed is related to being in the presence of God, maybe you need to surrender more of yourself and your time to bask in the presence of God daily, to sit at His feet and allow Him to teach you His truths, and to truly worship Him. Write out your thoughts that come from this self-examination.

_____

_____

_____

Meditate today on Matthew 2:10: "When they saw the star, they were overjoyed"(NIV). Throughout the day, ask God to help you be more aware of His presence in your life so that you can be overjoyed to such an extent that you worship Him and so that this joy will bring others to Him. Thank Him for sending His Son to be born in the flesh so that this joy is available to all who receive Him.

Notes

Day Twenty-One—Gifts

And going into the house, they saw the child with Mary his mother, and they fell down and worshiped him. Then, opening their treasures, they offered him gifts, gold and frankincense and myrrh.

—Matthew 2:11

Yesterday we discussed the joy that the Magi had from being in the presence of Jesus and how that joy led them to worship Him. Today, we will discuss the second result of the joy from being in the presence of Jesus, and that is the offering of gifts to Him.

Wycliffe's Commentary states that ancient commentators believed these gifts of the Magi—gold, frankincense, and myrrh—showed recognition of Jesus as King (gold), as Son of God (frankincense), and as one destined to die (myrrh). What this says to us, if we want to apply the same recognition of Jesus to our lives, is this: As King, He is our authority. As Son of God, He is the focus of our worship. As the one who died for us, He is our Savior, the focus of our love and service.

These gifts symbolize what our gifts to Jesus should be. The greatest gift we can give Jesus is ourselves, encompassing all of us that the gifts of the Magi symbolized.

As our authority, it's Jesus we should obey and strive to please. He is the one who has all the right to tell us what to do, and we must obey Him if we want to please Him. Give examples of ways you allow Jesus to be the authority in your everyday life.

_____

_____

As the Son of God, He's the focus of our worship, the one we should adore with all our heart, bowing our knees and our heart to Him in recognition of our lowliness and His glory. Worship is seeing ourselves as we really are and Him for who He really is. How would you describe your daily worship of Jesus?

_____

As our Savior, He should be the reason we live. We owe everything to Him. His saving us is the only reason we can truly live today and forever. How would you describe your living for Him? Are you living for yourself or for Him?

_____

In order for Jesus to be all these things to us, there must be a foundation and that foundation is found in Jesus's own words. One day during Jesus's ministry, one of the scribes approached Him and asked Him which commandment was the most important of all. Mark 12:29–31 records His answer: "[29]Jesus answered, 'The most important is, 'Hear, O Israel: The Lord our God, the Lord is one. [30]And you shall love the Lord your God with all your heart and with all your soul and with all your mind and with all your strength.' [31]The second is this: 'You shall love your neighbor as yourself.' There is no other commandment greater than these.'" There is probably no more fitting way to wrap up this study than to look at the significance of these words and see them as the best gift we can give Jesus on Christmas morning and every day of our lives. Let's look closely at these two commandments.

First, to love God with all your heart means that you adore Him above everyone else and everything else. Your heart is devoted to Him in such a way that your desire to please Him overrides everything you do. You long to spend time with Him, you long to know Him more, you're willing to sacrifice anything to please Him.

Second, to love God with all your soul means that you love Him from the very core of your being; your identity and your very existence are tied up in Him. Your soul is the real you, the you that will live forever. Your soul has a fleshly "house" for now, but when you cross over into heaven, your soul will be given a glorified body that you will have forever. This core that is called your soul is where your values come from, so when you love God with all your soul, your values reflect His values. Your core values direct your mind in the direction of pleasing God. At this level, God is not a part of your life—He *is* your life.

Third, to love God with all your mind means that your love for Him dictates that the decisions you make align with His will, that your choices are guided by Him and your thoughts are pleasing to Him. It also means that your mind craves knowledge gained from learning more about God's Word and wisdom to apply it to your life. Even further, it means that your mind's default is on Him and how you can please Him. You choose to meditate on His Word and allow it to saturate your being and control your thoughts and actions. A good test for how you measure up here is to notice where your mind goes when you're just in a mental "cruise" mode. Does it go to God or does it go to people or things?

Fourth, to love God with all your strength means to love Him with a passion that just automatically spills over into your countenance. People around you know without a doubt that you love Jesus, and you want to tell everyone else so they can know and love Him too. I'm convinced that if more of us loved Him with all our strength, more non-Christians would be won over to Him because they would be drawn to the excitement that He brings. We have a precious man in our church who is the embodiment of this commandment. His name is Richard Lewis, and you know as soon as you speak to Him that he loves Jesus and he wants to make sure you know and love Him as well. If only more of us could follow Richard's example! This really should be the norm for all of us Christians because we have a peace and joy that no others have— we have a relationship with *the God* of the universe who loves and cares for us.

If all our devotion, thoughts, decisions, and actions are centered around this commandment to love God with all our hearts, souls, minds, and strength, we will be pleasing to God, and we will bring honor and glory to Him—our King, the Son of God and our Savior.

In the previous passage, Jesus gave a second commandment: "You shall love your neighbor as yourself." Jesus's ministry was all about serving others, even to the point of laying down His life for all humanity. We would do well to emulate as fully as we can with the leadership and power of His Holy Spirit the servant attitude that He demonstrated. As the greatest teacher who ever lived, let us learn the very powerful lessons He taught and still today teaches through His Word and the Holy Spirit.

To wrap up these two love commandments and this study, let's look at one other passage that should help us understand what God desires from us. It comes from Romans 12:1: "I appeal to you therefore, brothers, by the mercies of God, to present your bodies as a living sacrifice, holy and acceptable to God, which is your spiritual worship." Our lives should literally be that of a living sacrifice that is holy and, therefore, acceptable and pleasing to God. **So the best gift we can give Jesus this Christmas and every day is ourselves—all of our heart, soul, mind and strength—to love Him, obey Him, fellowship with Him and serve Him.** We should give all that we are to all that He is, and we should live joyfully and unselfishly as we serve others. Then we will experience the true meaning of life and the abundant life that Jesus came to give us.

Meditate today on this part of Matthew 2:11: "Then, opening their treasures, they offered him gifts, gold and frankincense and myrrh." Throughout the day, ask God to help you give yourself completely to Him, loving Him with all your heart, soul, mind, and strength, and serving Him in whatever ways He directs. Develop a continual sense of worshiping Him as you go about your day. Also, thank Him for the greatest gift ever given—His sending His Son to be born in the flesh for the salvation of mankind.

Notes

Conclusion

Thank you for doing this Bible study. It is my prayer that you have truly been changed by the Christmas story and that this study has given your days leading up to Christmas special meaning that has impacted your mind and activities and made them more worshipful and Christ-centered than ever before. List below any thoughts that particularly caught your attention and anything that you want to put into practice from what you've studied. Also, feel free to email me any thoughts you have at sherry@sherrymyers.com. I would love to hear from you.

_____

_____

_____

_____

_____

_____

_____

_____

_____

_____

_____

_____

_____

Epilogue

Has this study challenged you to grow more in the likeness of Jesus? Have you been changed by the story of the birth of Jesus?

Has God given you an overriding desire to live in a way that prepares other people to hear about the life, death and resurrection of His precious Son, Jesus?

The goal of any Bible study should be to advance the Gospel of Jesus and His kingdom. The goal is not to help us live in a way that makes us look good to those around us, but to glorify Jesus and exalt Him in a way that draws people to Him. So it is my prayer that you didn't just "go through" this Bible study for your own good, but that you allowed God to write His Word on your heart in such a way that you are changed because of what He has done in you and that this change results in others coming to Christ because they see Him in you.

Our world seems to be in a mess on so many different levels right now, but I am convinced that if we Christians, instead of getting discouraged, will allow Jesus to live powerfully through us, many people will want Him because they will know His love and grace. Will you surrender your heart daily to carry His name in a way that reflects His character of love, forgiveness, grace, joy, and peace?

Consider the words of the apostle Peter recorded in Second Peter 1:3–4: "His divine power has granted to us all things that pertain to life and godliness, through the knowledge of him who called us to his own glory and excellence, by which he has granted to us his precious and very great promises, so that through them you may become partakers of the divine nature, having escaped from the corruption that is in the world because of sinful desire."

God bless you as you seek to live for Him and share Him with the lost around you.

Printed in the United States
By Bookmasters